'Halal is beautifully simple, yet complicated at the same time. Professor Tieman's skilled voice adds another vignette to the gestalt of this growing phenomenon'.
    - *Professor Jonathan A.J. Wilson, author of* Halal Branding

'This book is written by an expert who understands the complexity of halal and has widely contributed to the subject through his previous publications. *Halal Business Management* offers a practical guide for organisations and professionals serving Muslim markets'.
> - *Professor Mohammad Hashim Kamali, Professor and Founding CEO, International Institute of Advanced Islamic Studies, Malaysia*

'If you want to enrich your halal business management knowledge and experiences, you need this book. It gives proven, practical strategies to guide you and it has triggered fundamental improvement around the globe. The excellent ideas in this book are based on Dr. Marco Tieman's long experience as an international consultant and lecturer on halal supply chain management. This book is also reader-friendly and reflects the world of the practices while presented case studies offer inspiring models of halal excellence achievement'.
> - *Dr. H. Sapta Nirwandar, Vice Minister of Tourism and Creative Economy, Republic of Indonesia (2011–2014) and Chairman of Indonesia Halal Lifestyle Center*

'This publication is the first course outline for Halal Business Management to help decide whether or not to introduce halal certification, and the best practices connected to it, into your business plan; or how to excel at it if you are already halal certified. It also highlights the weak areas that need to be addressed, with emphasis on training throughout the organisation for end-to-end halal assurance. I would suggest beginning with the Epilogue where you can read the overview of the course, and then decide your answer to the final question: Are you ready for Halal Excellence?'

- *Salama Evans, Managing Editor, HalalFocus.com*

'*Halal Business Management* is a must-read comprehensive guide to excellence. Both newcomers and those already in business will find clear explanations and illustrative examples on the main topics related to halal trade. Starting with halal certification, which remains a topic of debate, the guide provides an overview of other, often neglected, but equally relevant issues, such as halal supply chain management, branding and marketing and the sensitive issue of halal risk and reputation, where Dr. Tieman shares his valuable expertise in the field. A much needed critical approach to this expanding market and its complexities'.

- *Dr. Barbara Ruiz-Bejarano, Instituto Halal*

'We are living in challenging times. The publication of *Halal Business Management* is both timely and necessary as we all seek guidance on how best to adapt and apply standards that are both relevant and implementable. Marco has produced a book that is both essential reading and impactful in its advice. This book will help us to embrace the change that will be a constant in the future'.

- *Daud Vicary, Managing Director, DVA Consulting Sdn. Bhd.*

'*Halal Business Management* is a must-read book for those operating in the global halal economy. From current supply chains to strategies in halal marketing, Dr. Marco Tieman guides the reader through a practical approach to working in this fast-growing market'.

- *Shakeeb Saqlain, CEO IslamicMarkets.com*

HALAL BUSINESS MANAGEMENT

The halal industry is a fast-growing industry due to demographics and industry expansion. Halal certification of products, outlets, and services is essential for doing business in Muslim-majority countries. This book shares the building blocks of professional halal business management, covering halal certification, halal supply chain management, branding and marketing, and halal risk and reputation management.

Drawing on years of academic research and advisory experience, the book provides practical advice and guidance on how best to organise and upscale your halal business operations. Successful companies in the halal industry are those that embrace halal excellence *by design*. Halal excellence is a process – a pursuit of excellence. Halal business management is beyond halal certification, and needs to address supply chain management, branding and marketing, and risk and reputation management. Halal excellence needs measurement through adopting the right key performance indicators, to protect your halal reputation and licence to operate in Muslim markets.

This book gives proven, practical strategies to guide you in the halal industry. The book is for all organisations involved in serving Muslim markets, and also serves as a coursebook for graduate and postgraduate education in halal business management.

Marco Tieman is the CEO of LBB International, a supply chain strategy consultancy and research firm. He is a professor with Help University and a research fellow with the Universiti Malaya Halal Research Centre, conducting research in halal supply chain management and reputation management.

HALAL BUSINESS MANAGEMENT

A Guide to Achieving Halal Excellence

Marco Tieman

LONDON AND NEW YORK

First published 2021
by Routledge
2 Park Square, Milton Park, Abingdon, Oxon OX14 4RN

and by Routledge
52 Vanderbilt Avenue, New York, NY 10017

Routledge is an imprint of the Taylor & Francis Group, an informa business

© 2021 Marco Tieman

The right of Marco Tieman to be identified as author of this work has been asserted by him in accordance with sections 77 and 78 of the Copyright, Designs and Patents Act 1988.

All rights reserved. No part of this book may be reprinted or reproduced or utilised in any form or by any electronic, mechanical, or other means, now known or hereafter invented, including photocopying and recording, or in any information storage or retrieval system, without permission in writing from the publishers.

Trademark notice: Product or corporate names may be trademarks or registered trademarks, and are used only for identification and explanation without intent to infringe.

British Library Cataloguing-in-Publication Data
A catalogue record for this book is available from the British Library

Library of Congress Cataloging-in-Publication Data

Names: Tieman, Marco, author.
Title: Halal business management : a guide to achieving halal excellence / Marco Tieman.
Description: Milton Park, Abingdon, Oxon ; New York, NY : Routledge, 2021. | Includes bibliographical references and index.
Identifiers: LCCN 2020029472 (print) | LCCN 2020029473 (ebook) | ISBN 9780367625870 (hardback) | ISBN 9780367625917 (paperback) | ISBN 9781003109853 (ebook)
Subjects: LCSH: Halal food industry--Management. | Halal food industry--Marketing.
Classification: LCC HD9334.A2 T54 2021 (print) | LCC HD9334.A2 (ebook) |
DDC 664.0068--dc23
LC record available at https://lccn.loc.gov/2020029472
LC ebook record available at https://lccn.loc.gov/2020029473

ISBN: 978-0-367-62587-0 (hbk)
ISBN: 978-0-367-62591-7 (pbk)
ISBN: 978-1-003-10985-3 (ebk)

Typeset in Joanna
by MPS Limited, Dehradun

CONTENTS

List of halal insights	ix
List of figures	x
List of tables	xii
Foreword	xiii
Acknowledgements	xvi
Prologue: A man with a mission	xvii
Arabic terms	xix

PART I: Halal certification — 1

1. The world of halal — 3
2. Halal assurance system — 17

PART II: Halal supply chain management — 31

3. The halal supply chain — 33
4. Halal purchasing — 53

5	Halal logistics and retailing	70
6	Halal clusters	88

PART III: Halal branding and marketing 105

7	Halal branding	107
8	Halal marketing	121

PART IV: Halal risk and reputation management 139

9	Halal risk management	141
10	Halal reputation management	156

Epilogue: A pursuit of excellence	173
Appendix 1: Halal certification information checklist	178
Appendix 2: Halal business management education	181
Appendix 3: Halal Reputation GAME	191
About the author	195
Index	197

LIST OF HALAL INSIGHTS

Halal Insight 1.1 Halal diets	6
Halal Insight 2.1 Halal Europe	20
Halal Insight 3.1 Halal supply chain definitions	38
Halal Insight 6.1 Halal Malaysia	98
Halal Insight 7.1 Halal trust measurement	110
Halal Insight 8.1 Shariah-compliant and Muslim-friendly hotel	131
Halal Insight 10.1 Cadbury Malaysia	157

LIST OF FIGURES

Figure 1.1 Halal industry is growing in width and depth	5
Figure 1.2 Halal according to the Hofstede onion diagram	8
Figure 1.3 Evolution of halal	9
Figure 1.4 Halal industry megatrends	11
Figure 2.1 HAS as module on top of your QMS	19
Figure 3.1 Foundation of halal supply chain management	34
Figure 3.2 Minimum versus preferred level in halal supply chain management	36
Figure 3.3 A halal supply chain network	37
Figure 3.4 Halal supply chain model	39
Figure 3.5 Supply chain partner classification	41
Figure 3.6 Halal supply chain design principles	44
Figure 3.7 Vertical collaboration	45

Figure 3.8	Horizontal collaboration	47
Figure 3.9	Halal blockchain	50
Figure 4.1	Halal compliance matrix	56
Figure 4.2	Halal purchasing function	58
Figure 4.3	The Kraljic Portfolio Matrix	60
Figure 4.4	Movements in the Kraljic Portfolio Matrix	61
Figure 4.5	Horizontal collaboration in purchasing	62
Figure 4.6	The Van Weele Purchasing Process	64
Figure 4.7	Halal supplier selection iceberg	66
Figure 5.1	Classification of halal logistics service providers	72
Figure 5.2	Halal standards for the halal logistics service provider	74
Figure 5.3	Halal warehouse processes	75
Figure 5.4	Halal transport processes	78
Figure 5.5	Halal compliant terminal process	81
Figure 6.1	Halal cluster model	91
Figure 6.2	Modern Halal Valley	102
Figure 7.1	Halal trust iceberg	109
Figure 7.2	Branding halal	114
Figure 7.3	Halal brand positioning matrix	117
Figure 9.1	Halal risk management control	145
Figure 9.2	Halal supply chain risk prevention cycle	147
Figure 9.3	Halal supply chain risk mitigation cycle	149
Figure 9.4	Halal supply chain risk recovery cycle	152
Figure 10.1	Halal reputation index	167
Figure 10.2	Halal reputation index indicators	167
Figure 10.3	Licence to operate rating	168
Figure 10.4	Halal reputation journey	170

LIST OF TABLES

Table 1.1	The halal maturity checklist	10
Table 2.1	Halal assurance system requirements	18
Table 2.2	Example of halal certification programme	24
Table 4.1	Halal procurement maturity model	55
Table 5.1	Halal control points and control measures in halal warehouse	76
Table 5.2	Halal control points and control measures in halal transport	79
Table 5.3	Halal control points and control measures in halal compliant terminal	82
Table 8.1	Marketing channel performance metrics (example)	125
Table 10.1	Halal issue classification	164

FOREWORD

My first doctorate is a PhD in Branding and my second doctorate is a DLitt in Halal, for a body of work grouped under the title: 'Being Hip and Halal, the Just Balance and the Floating World'. Halal also gave me an excuse to use my Chemistry and Life Sciences degree.

I have been cited for my contributions specifically in understanding halal's image and branding it, in various consumption patterns, Muslim voices, intersections with popular culture, geopolitics and ethnicity, and more broadly halal's philosophical underpinnings and the subsequent socio-business implications in a modern context.

I share all of this to give readers a preliminary insight into how: firstly, halal is now an established subject field and one that requires interdisciplinary expertise rooted in theory and practice; and secondly, that the field of halal has broadened and moved forward beyond what I term *'Meat and Money'*.

'Who the Halal are these foreigners, why are they here, and what do they know?'

This is the point where I introduce Professor Marco Tieman. Over nearly a decade, we got to know each other on the international conference circuit – watching each other speak, hanging out at various halal corporate dinner functions and after dark in hotel lounges. Not a particularly rock and roll lifestyle, but being completely honest, I will say that the two of us still stuck out simply for looking different, being taller than the average delegate, having Western names, and for trying to shake things up.

Over the years, Marco has answered those questions – by walking the hard yards and dedicating himself to the domain of halal with patience and humility. He received his doctorate in halal and has published a number of highly-cited academic journal papers in the field of Halal Supply Chain Management – which have bolstered his credentials as an industry consultant. Also, he has been a tireless servant of the *Journal of Islamic Marketing*, for which I am Editor-In-Chief. Marco is a Senior Advisory Board member for the journal and continues to peer-review perhaps more papers than he would like to – but this is both testament to his commitment and an indicator of how rapidly the field of halal is growing in scholarly and industry circles.

Nevertheless, halal markets, in many ways, are in their infancy. Furthermore, there is evidence to suggest that consumers and firms are split in their interpretation of this Arabic word. Regardless of their religious beliefs, some see halal as a mark of additional scrutiny or even added quality, but sadly others perceive that it may mean the exact opposite. Now that halal has arrived, in terms of being a logoed, labelled cluster of industries necessitating certification and robust end-to-end processes: this is where scholars and practitioners require more detailed consideration – if halal is to move from strength to strength and overcome some of the hurdles and negative perceptions. Whether that is farm to fork, or the more aspirational and experiential, halal has reached a critical point of reflection as to how alternative or complementary strategic business approaches can be developed further.

All too often, discussions on halal focus on permissibility and compliance – and these values are championed by halal certifiers, religious clergy, and journalists. Established players, aspiring entrepreneurs, and businesspeople are led to the gateway of markets, enticed by media reports of large numbers indicating growth potential – however less is said specifically about how to walk through these gateways and capitalise on such opportunities. It is one thing to identify a market and enter it, however, it requires different insight and expertise to be able to secure and maintain individual business growth.

This is why I believe Professor Tieman's book fills a gap and makes a valuable contribution towards providing answers to some of these questions. It provides clear explanations in key areas and useful exercises, designed to offer a structured approach to building businesses fit for serving halal markets.

Halal is beautifully simple, yet complicated at the same. Therefore, I was really pleased to hear from Marco about his intentions to write this book and honoured to be invited to support it with a foreword. His skilled voice adds another vignette to the gestalt of this growing phenomenon, where still more practical guidance and innovative thinking is required. Whether you are a business professional, educator, or researcher interested in the business of halal, there's something here to give you a grounding in the fundamentals.

Professor Jonathan A.J. Wilson PhD DLitt

ACKNOWLEDGEMENTS

I would like to thank the LBB International Malaysia and Indonesia team, who conducted research and spent hours brainstorming. Thank you to all our clients, governments, and the private sector, all over the world that allowed us to grow our halal business and our halal research centre.

Thank you shariah experts, halal experts, and industry experts, who I met over the years in sharing insights that made my academic research and this book achievable. Thank you Salama Evans for your support, ideas, and review.

Last but not least, I would like to thank the team at Routledge, Rebecca Marsh, Sophie Peoples, and Neema Sangmo Lama who made it possible to share Halal Business Management with the world.

I love you all!

PROLOGUE: A MAN WITH A MISSION

On a hot and sunny day in early 2006, I met Abdalhamid Evans for a casual lunch meeting at a restaurant in Taman Tun Dr Ismail, an upmarket district of Kuala Lumpur where I had my office at that time. A tall slim British man with a thin beard was sitting inside the restaurant next to the window. As I entered the restaurant, he greeted me with a warm smile. This must be him! We introduced each other, sit down, and the waitress came to take our order. Before explaining the reason why he wanted to see me, he asked me about how long I had lived in Malaysia and what I did before in the Netherlands. Once the food was served, he shared with me that he was advising the Malaysian Government to make Malaysia the global halal hub. As I explained my work in the area of supply chain management and cluster development in Europe and Asia, he concluded 'We need you to be part of our team!'. I told him 'I am not a Muslim and know very little about the halal industry'. He smiled and said: 'Marco, we need your expertise on supply chain management and cluster design in building this halal hub. Please come and visit our office next week, so I can introduce you to our team'. After my meeting in their Kuala Lumpur office, I accepted helping him. This was the start of a great journey and true friendship.

As Abdalhamid Evans invited me into the world of halal and showed me the beauty of Islam, I was searching for existing knowledge on the topic of halal supply chain management and halal clusters. But there was ... none! As I wanted to do my PhD but only if I could find a field of study where I could make an academic impact and at the same time a research area of use to my firm, an academic research into the application of halal in supply chain management was a gift straight from Heaven.

Late 2006, I started my PhD research with Universiti Teknologi MARA in Malaysia on the application of halal in supply chain management. In 2008, Abdalhamid Evans and business partners came back to me again to ask if I would be willing to chair the development of an international halal standard for logistics under the International Halal Integrity Alliance. I accepted this new challenge and the halal logistics standard was launched two years later in the year 2010. Upon completion of my PhD in 2013, I continued my academic research in the area of halal supply chain management and more recently on halal risk and reputation management.

Over the years together with my LBB International team, we helped governments and private sectors in halal certification, halal supply chain management, halal cluster development, and halal risk & reputation management. We became missionaries in sharing knowledge about halal business management through publications, guest lectures at universities, and speaking at conferences in Asia, the Middle East, and Europe. Hence, it became my personal mission to bring *Halal Excellence* to the world!

ARABIC TERMS

Fatwa: Religious ruling
Halal: Things or actions that are permissible or lawful under shariah
Haram: Things or actions that is prohibited or unlawful under shariah
Ihsan: Excellence
Kiblah: The direction that should be faced when a Muslim prays during his salat (prayers). The Kiblah should face the Kaabah, in the city of Mecca
Medium najis: Alcoholic beverages; halal livestock that is not halal slaughtered, and their derivates
Mizan: Living in balance with nature
Najis: Matters that are impure according to shariah. For halal supply chain management, it is important to differentiate between medium najis and severe najis
Niyyah: Intention
Non-halal: Things or actions that are not classified as halal

Quran: The Word of God as revealed to His Prophet Muhammad (PBUH)
Sertu: Ritual cleansing
Severe najis: Dog, pig, and their derivatives
Shariah: Islamic law
Sunnah: Historical collection of the Prophet Muhammad (PBUH) actions, sayings, and tacit approval
Tayyib: Good, wholesome

PART I

HALAL CERTIFICATION

1
THE WORLD OF HALAL

Introduction to halal

A significant paradigm shift in modern marketing is taking place, from a consumer-centric to a value-driven approach (Kotler et al. 2010), requiring the integration of Islamic values into business operations when operating in and/or exporting to predominantly Muslim countries.

Halal, which means 'lawful' (Al-Qaradawi 2007) has its origin from the holy Quran which tells humanity:

> *'O you people! Eat of what is on earth, lawful and good; and do not follow the footsteps of the Evil One, for he is to you an avowed enemy'*
>
> Quran (2:168)

In the holy Quran lawful (halal) and good (tayyib) always comes together as two sides of the same coin. Therefore, when we talk about halal excellence it connotes an equal emphasis on quality excellence. The Arabic term for excellence, perfection, or beautification is 'ihsan' (or ehsan). Ihsan is also the Muslim responsibility to obtain excellence in worship, and it also constitutes the highest form of worship. Ihsan is excellence in work and in social interactions, in both deed and action. Simply put, Ihsan is the pursuit of excellence.

My dear friend Abdalhamid Evans defined halal during one of his inspiring speeches at the World Halal Forum in Malaysia as follows:

> *'It is a portion of God's gift to mankind; lawful, wholesome, safe, healthy, pleasing. Halal is not just about the end product; it is the entire process. It is a trust, an honour, and a responsibility'*
>
> Abdalhamid Evans (1951–2018)

From his definition, we can identify four important lessons. First, halal goes beyond the technical meaning of 'lawful'. Halal requires an equal focus on wholesomeness, safety, health, and aesthetics. Second, halal should not be limited to only a product approach. Halal requires a process approach: end-to-end. Third, halal is related to trust which should be protected through standards and regulations. Fourth, halal is an honour and responsibility not only to consume, but also to provide (*read:* produce) so that humanity has access to products and services that are lawful and good.

Halal, rooted in shariah (Islamic law), is an important concept for Muslims to protect man from evil and to benefit mankind in all aspects of life (Al-Qaradawi, 2007). The opposite of halal is haram, meaning forbidden. The haram foods are mainly pork, alcohol, blood, dead animals, and animals slaughtered while reciting a name other than that of God. This includes also halal items that have been contaminated or mixed with haram items (Riaz and Chaudry, 2004). These things are prohibited due to their impurity and harmfulness.

The halal food laws in Islam provide important dietary guidelines for the daily life of Muslims. Some better insights into halal diets are shared below in Halal Insight 1.1.

However, halal is not limited to dietary regulations alone. Halal touches on all aspects of Muslim life. As a result, halal standards and certification have moved beyond food and have matured into non-food sectors such as services.

Today, the halal industry is a multi-trillion USD industry consisting of food, cosmetics, home care, pharmaceuticals, medical devices, chemicals, fashion, hospitality, finance and insurance, logistics, and many more. The halal industry is expanding rapidly as the industry grows in both width and depth (figure 1.1). The halal industry is expanding in width as new industries are seeking halal compliance and are getting halal

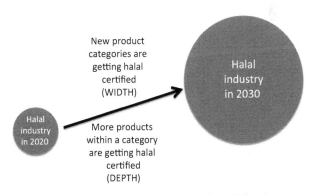

Figure 1.1 Halal industry is growing in width and depth.

Halal Insight 1.1 Halal diets

God encourages humans to conduct research on their food and says: 'Then let men look at his food, (and how We provide it)' (Quran 80:24). The Prophet (PBUH) frequently emphasised the medicinal properties of plants and the importance of various foods. According to the holy Quran, an important staple of our diet is water, corn, olives, date-palms, grapes, and every kind of fruit (Quran 6:99; 16:10–11; 23:19; 80:24–32). Olives, date-palms, and grapes have proven extensive medical properties. Most important fruit plants from the holy Quran are identified based on the number of times it was mentioned in the Holy Quran and also the order from other fruit plants: date palm, grape, olive, pomegranate, jujube, banana, and fig.

10 fruit plant species are explicitly mentioned in the Holy Quran and Hadith, namely: watermelon, cucumber, quince, figs, olive, date-palm, pomegranate, mustard tree, grapes, and jujube. The holy Quran also mentions the use of vegetable oil for food (Quran 23:20). The Prophet (PBUH) has said: 'Use the olive oil in your meals and also use it for massages. For this oil is obtained from a tree full of blessings'. Current research shows that the use of (extra virgin) olive oil in our daily diet, which is also associated with the Mediterranean diet, has plenty of health benefits.

It is the law of God that the lower order of species be sacrificed for the benefit of those that are above. Therefore, green plants are fed to an animal (and not other animals), and slaughtered for consumption to be food for man. Although it is still being debated to this day, various scientists believe that the mad cow disease was caused by animal feed, where cattle feed has been commonly supplemented with meat and bone meal made from animal carcasses.

A human's body is like a container, it can only fit in certain things and it is limited! So, fill your stomach with correct serving proportions as taught by the Prophet (PBUH) so we

> can be healthy: 1/3 food, 1/3 water, and 1/3 air for breathing. In other words, moderation is important for a healthy diet!
>
> The Ramadan is a 29–30 day fast in which food, fluids, medications, drugs, and smoking are prohibited during the daylight hours which can be between 13- and 18-hours per day depending on the geographical location and season. Today scientific evidence shows the benefits of fasting for healthy aging (Greger 2019, Verburgh 2018).
>
> The current food supply chain is characterised by high levels of waste in postharvest handling storage, processing and packaging, distribution, and consumption. The holy Quran is clear 'Eat and drink: but waste not by excess, for God loves not the wasters' (Quran 7:31).
>
> *Source: Tieman 2016*

certified. On the other hand, the halal industry is expanding in-depth, meaning more companies within one industry are getting halal certified. The demographics and economic development in Asia and the Middle East make the halal industry one you cannot afford to ignore. Halal is moving away from a niche market and into the mainstream, available in both predominantly Muslim and non-Muslim countries (Evans and Syed 2015).

As halal is moving mainstream, halal as a concept cannot be fully expressed within the construct of a product or service. It can be argued that halal reaches much further into the discipline of management, cultural anthropology, and sociology. If you describe halal from a cultural perspective, using the Hofstede (1991) onion diagram, 'halal' and its Arabic character becomes for Muslims an important 'symbol'. In Islam the Prophet Muhammad (PBUH) is the best role model ('hero') to emulate and follow; which actions, sayings, and tacit approval have been documented in the Sunnah (Laldin 2006). Islam has various 'rituals', such as

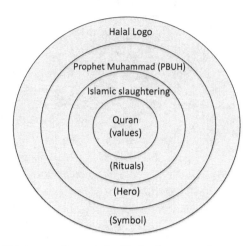

Figure 1.2 Halal according to the Hofstede onion diagram.

the method of ritual slaughter, and for certain Islamic schools of thought, there is also ritual cleansing. The core 'values' of Islam are based on the Holy Quran. Figure 1.2 presents the adoption of the Hofstede onion diagram to describe halal.

Halal is not static, but goes through an evolution (figure 1.3) from a Muslim company (purely based on a system of mutual trust between people), halal product (product is halal certified by an independent halal certification body), halal supply chain (a supply chain approach towards halal), to a halal value chain (halal is addressed throughout the entire business value chain) (Tieman 2011).

Several predominantly Muslim countries, with advanced halal standards like Malaysia, Indonesia, and the Middle East, are moving towards Stage 3: a halal supply chain. Stage 4, the halal value chain, might still take about ten years for Muslim majority countries to reach. One of the bottlenecks is Islamic banking and finance.

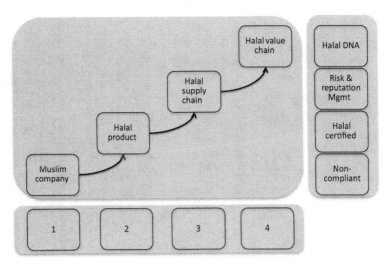

Figure 1.3 Evolution of halal.

The Islamic banking and finance sector has not matured yet as it still needs to address two major problems. First, international transactions for making international payments are not shariah compliant yet. Second, the full range of finance-banking-insurance needs for businesses is not available with a shariah-compliant alternative. Fortunately, in Muslim countries in Asia and the Middle East, there are universities involved in academic research that are working on strengthening the shariah compliance of this sector.

The evolution of halal as a concept can also be used for an organisation in assessing the halal maturity of a company. Halal maturity is hereby defined as the main position of an organisation in the halal evolution. The fact that a company has an Islamic bank account does not automatically mean that the position of the company is already at Level 4 (Halal Value Chain). In order to reach Level 4, your organisation also needs to be fully compliant with Level 2 (Halal Product) and Level 3 (Halal Supply Chain). The halal maturity checklist is shown in table 1.1. By answering ten questions in the checklist, it will define the current main position of your organisation: your halal maturity. The halal maturity of a company could be introduced as a key performance indicator, or objective, for top management of companies operating in and exporting to Muslim majority countries. A higher level of halal maturity results in more effective risk and reputation management when doing business in Muslim majority countries.

In summary, the halal industry is fast-growing and dynamic. Megatrends in the halal industry are: (1) next to food, also non-food needs to be halal certified; (2) similar to food safety, halal requires a supply chain approach: end-to-end; and (3) the need for halal risk and reputation management (figure 1.4).

Table 1.1 The halal maturity checklist

#	Question	YES	NO	
1	Does your organisation have a Halal Assurance System (HAS) manual?			Any NO-s? -> LEVEL 1: MUSLIM COMPANY
2	Is your organisation halal certified by a Halal Certification Body?			The halal status of the product/service is assumed based on trust between the buyer and seller. However, strengthen your HAS to ensure compliance with industry needs and market requirements from Muslim markets.
3	Are your operations, purchasing and logistics staff trained on halal?			

All YES?: continue with question 4

#	Question	YES	NO	
4	Does your HAS cover transport and storage requirements for all ingredient/product component sourcing and in distribution of your final product?			Any NO-s? -> LEVEL 2: HALAL PRODUCT
5	Do these sourcing & distribution contracts have a halal clause, and is halal covered during the audit of supply chain partners?			The basis for trust is the halal logo from a Halal Certification Body, which ensures the halal integrity of ingredients/components and operational processes. However, protect your licence-to-operate in Muslim markets by addressing the emerging requirements of a Halal Supply Chain.
6	Does your organisation have a halal supply chain risk prevention, risk mitigation, and risk recovery plan?			

All YES?: continue with question 7

#	Question	YES	NO	
7	Does your organisation have Islamic branding & marketing guidelines?			Any NO-s? -> LEVEL 3: HALAL SUPPLY CHAIN
8	Has your organisation replaced animal with plant-based ingredients/components where possible?			Halal risk and reputation management is addressed by your organisation throughout your supply chain: end-to-end. You have a professional HAS in place, protecting the corporate halal reputation of your organisation. Your next challenge is to draft a strategy and action plan to move halal towards a Halal Value Chain.
9	Does your organisation have a green policy in place, covering: waste reduction, green energy (solar, wind), and water management (usage + pollution)?			
10	Does your organisation use Islamic banking and Takaful where possible?			

All YES? -> LEVEL 4: HALAL VALUE CHAIN

Halal requirements are addressed throughout your corporate value chain, assuring a correct-consistent-complete-clear corporate Halal DNA. A Halal DNA provides the best foundation for a premium halal brand. The Halal Value Chain is the highest level of halal maturity a company can reach. Congratulations, well done! You are one of the few companies that have reached level 4.

Figure 1.4 Halal industry megatrends.

Control of halal chains

A large extent of global agriculture produce, ranging from meat and dairy to grains, vegetables, and fruits is supplied by big farms from Europe, Australia and New Zealand, and the Americas. Most Muslim countries are net-importers of agriculture produce. Muslim majority countries are very much dependent on the supply of their food resources from non-Muslim countries, and consequently, their food security is of great concern. As most food ingredients and additives companies are located in these farming clusters, the production of food ingredients and additives is concentrated in non-Muslim countries.

Today many ingredients and additives have components that are of animal origin. For halal products, this immediately leads to a halal issue. Like human beings, animals are creatures of God, and thus they have life. As a result, in Islam, the consumption of meat is prohibited unless it meets very high standards in animal slaughter and animal welfare. Hence, the legal purification of the flesh of animals for consumption requires strict conditions in Islam (Al-Qaradawi 2007). Halal authorities have immediate questions on what animal (whether or not it is from halal livestock), what part of the animal (meat, bone, hair, etc.), what method of slaughtering (halal slaughtered, machine slaughtered, stunned), what type of halal certification granted, and so on.

Although commodity markets facilitate supply and demand for agriculture commodities, only a fraction of the supply has been halal certified. With an enormous increase of halal-certified producers all over the world, the demand for halal raw materials, ingredients, and additives has grown faster than the supply can cope with. This leads to major challenges for halal-certified producers in sourcing the required halal-certified raw materials, ingredients, and additives, often resulting in higher prices. The supply of halal-certified ingredients and additives is a definite bottleneck for the halal industry in increasing the production of halal food for the world.

Although the halal requirements for food are an important factor for Muslims, it previously did not translate into a dominant role of the Organisation of Islamic Cooperation (OIC) member countries. Most OIC countries have food security issues, there is a limited role and underinvestment in the halal food value chain in order to protect availability and access to halal food. Although it can be argued that the Muslim world does not have a competitive advantage for many agriculture commodities owing to their geographic locations, there have been too few attempts to extend the role of OIC countries in the halal value chain.

Urgent investments are needed to develop capacity in halal supply chains and addressing the most critical bottlenecks in the halal (food) supply chain, namely in the production of halal-certified (food) ingredients and additives. Islamic banks could play a key role in financing these projects together with governments and industry. Islamic countries need to draft halal industry strategies to better organise and upscale halal production, reducing dependence on the import from other (often non-Muslim) countries and avoiding food shortages.

On the other hand, non-Muslim countries and industries from non-Muslim countries need clear guidelines on halal. Therefore, urgent consensus is needed by the Muslim world on commonalities and differences among the different halal requirements. This agreement should lead to the coding of the different halal specifications, making halal requirements & differences transparent to both industry and consumers. As consensus is a long process, the protection of halal is needed in non-Muslim countries. Although many non-Muslim countries do not protect halal by law, halal disclosure laws, which requires a vendor who claims that a product is halal to show the basis of the claim, this could be a good first step in this direction. A labelling law is a second practical method of protecting the halal logo on products in the market place in non-Muslim countries, similar to organic labels.

Halal excellence philosophy

The pursuit of halal excellence is a process. If you want to successfully operate in and export to Muslim markets, business leaders should embrace the halal excellence philosophy.

The core purpose of businesses embracing a halal excellence philosophy is to serve humanity with products and services that are lawful and good. There are seven (7) main principles to embracing the halal excellence philosophy:

- **No compromises** on inputs (ingredients, equipment, and people) and processes. In a world of compromise, excellence in all facets in business management and operations wins (chapter 2).
- **Halal excellence by design** based on correct-consistent-complete-clear (Geijn 2005) halal assurance system (chapter 2), halal supply chain management (chapters 3–6), halal branding and marketing (chapters 7 and 8), and halal risk

and reputation management (chapters 9 and 10). Efforts put in here will definitely return investments.
- **Practise and repetition** of the halal assurance system, halal risk management control, and halal reputation management. Practise makes perfect is not only true for musicians and sportsmen, but also in halal business management (chapters 2, 9, and 10).
- **Effective command and control of your halal supply chain and corporate halal reputation**. Excellence in halal supply chains requires the right key performance indicators to measure the effectiveness, efficiency, and robustness of your halal supply chain (chapter 3). Excellence in corporate halal reputation requires measurement of the halal reputation index and licence to operate rating (chapter 10).
- **Having the best team**. The staff in your company, but also your supply chain partners, and external stakeholders (chapters 2–6). Realise that competition today is no longer between companies, but between supply chain networks. Continuous training and education on halal are essential, not only for the organisation but also for its supply chain. Strategic alliances and associations are critical for doing successful business in the Muslim world.
- **Engagement with your customer**. Customer service is not a department but everybody's job. Co-create your products and services together with your customers (chapter 6–8). Honesty and transparency with your customer are important values, not only during good times but also during a halal issue and crisis (chapters 9 and 10).
- **In balance with nature (*mizan*)**. Everything in creation is made to exist in perfect balance. This delicate balance is not to be disturbed (chapter 6).

This book will provide the reader with halal business management strategies, tactics, and best operational practices to implement halal excellence into your organisation and supply chain network. Welcome to the world of halal.

Summary – chapter 1: The world of halal

- Halal requires an equal and deliberate focus on quality. Halal necessitates, similar to food safety, a process approach: end-to-end
- Halal is not static, it is moving away from a product approach and towards a supply chain and value chain approach
- Ingredients and additives are an important bottleneck in the fast-growing halal industry
- The core purpose of industries embracing a halal excellence philosophy is to serve humanity with products and services that are lawful and good

Reflection questions

- How can you improve your image or competitive advantage in predominantly Muslim countries?
- What is the value of halal certification for doing business in your local and export markets?
- What problems can your company solve in the halal industry?

References

Al-Qaradawi, Y., 2007. The Lawful and the Prohibited in Islam. Islamic Book Trust, Petaling Jaya.

Evans, A., Syed, S., 2015. From Niche to Mainstream: Halal Goes Global. International Trade Centre, Geneva.

Geijn, R. van, 2005. Natural Business Excellence. Align Group, Bangkok.

Greger, M., 2019. How Not to Diet: The Groundbreaking Science of Healthy, Permanent Weight Loss. Bluebird, London.

Hofstede, G., 1991. Cultures and Organisations: Software of the Mind: Intercultural Cooperation and Its Importance for Survival. Harper Collins, London.

Laldin, M. A., 2006. Islamic Law – An introduction. Research Centre - International Islamic University Malaysia, Kuala Lumpur.

Kotler, P, Kartajaya, H., Setiawan, I., 2010. Marketing 3.0: From products to Customers to the Human Spirit. John Wiley & Sons, Inc, Hoboken.

Riaz, M. N., Chaudry, M. M., 2004. Halal Food Production. CRC Press, Boca Raton.

Tieman, M., 2011. The application of Halal in supply chain management: in-depth interviews. Journal of Islamic Marketing 2 (2), 186–195. https://doi.org/10.1108/17590831111139893.

Tieman, M., 2016. Halal diets. Islam and Civilisational Renewal 7 (1), 128–132.

Verburgh, K., 2018. The Longevity Code: Secrets to Living Well for Longer from the Front Lines of Science. The Experiment, LLC, New York.

2

HALAL ASSURANCE SYSTEM

Introduction to halal assurance systems (HAS)

The fast-growing global halal market is supported by strong economic fundamentals where new categories of halal-certified products (and services), more stringent halal requirements for ingredients, and more Islamic countries developing halal standards are shaping the global halal industry. This fast expansion of the halal industry has led to a high demand for halal certification services.

A halal assurance system (HAS) is an integrated management system which is developed, implemented and maintained to

manage purchasing, production/processing, materials handling, distribution, and other services in accordance with a halal standard.

A halal standard specifies the requirements of halal certification by a halal certification body (HCB). The most common HAS requirements are listed in table 2.1.

The basis or backbone of your halal assurance system (HAS) is your quality management system (QMS). HAS does not replace your QMS, but sits as a module on top of your QMS (figure 2.1). In fact, your HAS refers to your QMS processes. If you have a sound QMS in place, a halal certification programme is much easier when compared to a typical ISO or HACCP implementation programme.

Table 2.1 Halal assurance system requirements

Process	Product ingredients/components allowed
	Primary packaging materials allowed
	Production process and materials handling requirements
	Storage and transport requirements
Control	Halal Assurance System (HAS) manual requirements
	Operations facility requirements
	Handling of complaints and feedback
	Non-conformance handling
	Management review
	List of approved foreign halal certification bodies recognised by your halal certification body or bodies (in case multiple halal certification bodies need to be used)
Organisation	Halal policy (statement)
	Halal committee
	Internal halal audit
	Halal training and education
Information	Traceability
	Labelling of the halal logo on the product/outlet/service
	Marking/coding of the halal status on cargo labels, freight documents, and IT systems
	Method and frequency of communication with the halal certification body

Figure 2.1 HAS as module on top of your QMS.

The halal certification body (HCB)

The number of halal certification bodies (HCBs) worldwide is estimated at around 400–500. The exact number is difficult to obtain because there is no international or Organisation of Islamic Cooperation (OIC) registration database of HCBs. In predominantly Muslim countries, the HCB is usually a government department (like BPJPH in Indonesia and JAKIM in Malaysia), whereas in non-Muslim countries the HCB is a company, non-government organisation, or unit within a mosque. Some non-Muslim countries like Singapore and Thailand have a Halal Act, whereby the government accredits the HCB, but most countries do not have this bill. This has led to a wide spectrum in competency levels of HCBs available in non-Muslim countries, like in Europe where there is limited government control on halal matters (Halal Insight 2.1).

Non-Muslim countries need to understand that halal, albeit originally with religious foundations, touches on various important government regulations similar to other credence quality attributes like organic and fair trade, which non-Muslim countries have been regulating. A reactive approach towards halal requirements is dangerous for non-Muslim countries, as it is dependent on exporting products to the Muslim world. In order

Halal Insight 2.1 Halal Europe

Compared to the rest of the world, Europe has one of the toughest food quality, product quality, and safety standards which you need to comply with when producing in or exporting to the European market. Therefore, the European Government, in principle, has created a solid foundation for a halal system.

Halal is regarded in Europe and its member states as a purely religious matter, in which the government does not want to get involved. The argument is based on the custom of 'separation of church and state'. As a result, halal certification is left to the private sector without any arm's length of control from central or local governments. To illustrate, there are no requirements to set up a halal certification company, there is no accreditation from the central or local government of a halal certification body, Europe has no halal standard or guidelines in place, and the halal logo is not protected by any kind of regulation.

This liberal halal policy has led to a proliferation of many private halal certification bodies in Europe. Some of these certification bodies have a solid halal certification system based on a transparent halal standard and is supported by a solid auditing mechanism. Unfortunately, many do not follow this system. This affected the reputation of the entire halal certification sector in Europe, thus impeding the potential of 'Halal Europe' as a premium halal brand.

Halal is a credence quality attribute, meaning that these characteristics are not visible and verifiable by the consumer, until experts or other professional services reveal them. Similar to other credence quality attributes like organic, fair trade, and kosher, the halal status is communicated to the consumer through a halal logo on the packaging or to the industrial buyer as a halal certificate. Europe has one of the most stringent food and nutrition labelling laws in the world, which also apply to the

> credence logos of organic and fair-trade products, but surprisingly do not apply to religious logos such as halal and kosher. This has resulted in various halal issues in Europe, for example, many fake halal logos on food products are in retail, fake halal logos are used by restaurants and fast-food outlets, and halal certificates with export shipments to predominantly Muslim countries without any halal assurance system in place for the company concerned.
>
> *Source: Tieman 2017*

to protect its halal export interest, non-Muslim countries should shift from a reactive approach to a proactive approach.

Each HCB has its own unique halal standard and interpretation of requirements of halal certification shaped by their Islamic school of thought, fatwas (Islamic rulings), and local customs. Although there have been various attempts at harmonisation, even among neighbouring Islamic countries within the same Islamic school of thought (like Indonesia, Malaysia, and Brunei), there can be significant differences observed particularly in halal slaughtering requirements, alcohol percentage allowed (in ingredients), determining which ingredients require halal certification, and which foreign halal certification bodies are recognised.

In fact, you could even argue that HCBs do not even recognise each other. Some HCBs, such as BPJPH in Indonesia and JAKIM in Malaysia, create lists of which other HCBs they recognise for meat slaughtering, raw materials, flavours, and perfumes. However, when it comes to slaughtering, HCBs recognise slaughterhouses only once their own HCB has personally inspected the slaughterhouse. Hence, selecting the right halal certification body, given your business and export goals, is therefore not an easy task. In case you make use of multiple HCBs certifying your factory, which is a common practice among multinational food companies, this will lead to major complexities for your purchasing department.

The main reason is that there are inconsistencies between the halal certification standards in terms of halal slaughtering requirements, use of certain ingredients, allowed alcohol percentage (in ingredients), and foreign halal certification bodies recognised. Developing the right halal certification strategy is crucial in making halal simple and sustainable for your operations given your business and export goals.

Halal requirements for certification are not static, it is continuously developing based on the new insights of the HCB. New insights are triggered by consensus among HCBs, new fatwas, and revision of the HCB halal standards (every 5–10 years). Therefore, for a robust halal assurance system, it is critical to design a halal assurance system that not only complies with the current minimum requirements, but also accounts for emerging future requirements. Failure to do this will lead to an unstable halal assurance system, with a high risk of losing your halal certificate for a period of time. A major problem is the reality that HCBs typically give little time to comply with a new halal requirement. Hence, it is recommended to recruit a halal expert in designing and implementing your halal assurance system. Meeting the minimum certification requirements will result in a lot of fire-fighting and potential loss of attractive export markets. As will be discussed in chapter 10, losing your halal certificate has serious consequences on corporate reputation.

Key activities undertaken by HCBs are providing (1) information; (2) testimony; (3) judgement or decree; (4) authority; and (5) general dealings and transactions (Shah 2017). Islamic law requires that providing information about the halal and haram must be done by two competent Muslims. For testimonies and witnesses, all schools of Islamic thought require this to be done by a Muslim who is mature, of sound mind, just, and a free person. For a judge they must be a Muslim who is mature, sound of mind, just, free, physically healthy, secure from slander, have the absolute power to issue a decree, and is not deaf, mute, or blind. For the supervision of Muslim affairs, the one in-charge must be a competent Muslim. For general dealings and transactions, a reliable and proficient person, not necessarily a Muslim, is enough. As a result, halal certification bodies are controlled by Muslims in both predominantly Muslim and non-Muslim countries.

Steps in halal certification

A halal certification programme typically follows four steps: halal strategy, 0-base assessment, HAS documentation, and implementation as shown in table 2.2. The lead-time of a halal certification programme depends on the complexity of the certification programme, support from suppliers in submitting the necessary documentation, red item management, and the efficiency of the HCB process. Let me discuss each step in more detail.

Halal strategy

The halal strategy is a plan of action designed to achieve halal excellence. As halal moves away from a product approach and towards a supply chain and value chain approach, you must establish a solid purchasing-production-materials handling-distribution strategy. Second, as will be discussed in chapters 7 and 8, in order to build and protect your halal brand, correct halal branding and marketing strategy is needed to ensure alignment with the Islamic values of your key Muslim markets.

The halal certification strategy determines which halal standard or combination of halal standards are used in the planning of the halal certification programme. The choice of halal standard(s) is based on your business and export goals. However, halal certification itself is a risk management decision as it is related to your

Table 2.2 Example of halal certification programme

Halal strategy	Halal purchasing-production-materials handling-distribution strategy
	Halal branding & marketing strategy
	Halal certification strategy
	Corporate halal policy
0-base assessment	Assess all ingredients/materials of products using the halal production lines
	Red item management of materials with a halal issue, which need to be discussed with the halal authority, replaced with an alternative ingredient or supplier, etc.
	Assess receiving, production, materials handling, and distribution
HAS documentation	Organisation design
	Facility design specification
	Halal Assurance System (HAS) documentation design
Implementation	Training of Halal Committee
	Training of staff
	Preparation of halal operations
	Application with Halal Certification Body (HCB)
	Conduct internal halal audit by consultant
	Conduct external halal audit by HCB

licence to operate in predominantly Muslim countries. The HCB chosen has a significant impact on the complexity of your HAS and export reach. Be careful in using multiple halal standards as this increases your complexity of HAS exponentially. For large and multinational companies, the phasing of halal brands needs to be determined: which brands come first, which brands come later?

Some key considerations in the phasing of halal brands:

- **Destination country:** predominantly Muslim country first, non-Muslim country later?
- **Volume:** high-volume mass-market brands first, low-volume specialised brands later?

- **Animal-based:** non-animal based brands and products first, animal-based brands and products later?
- **Food versus non-food:** food brands and products that go into the mouth first, non-food brands and products that do not go into the mouth later?
- **Complexity of production:** simple products first, complex products later? Single production sites first, multiple production sites later?

Halal certification goes by brand. You cannot have part of a brand product range halal-certified, whereas the rest of a product range is not yet halal certified at retail level available in a single predominantly Muslim country. We work for multinational companies, where one brand is manufactured in multiple factories based in different countries. You can only carry the halal certificate on a brand when all factories are halal certified. The company might also have a manufacturing unit for flavours or fragrances which are part of the ingredients of a brand. You can also have important ingredient suppliers that require halal certification under a specific halal standard that are currently not halal-certified or are certified by the 'wrong' HCB. These certification projects will need to be undertaken in parallel. In short, a halal certification programme could involve parallel certification projects of multiple sites and multiple companies. The longest certification lead-time of a halal certification project will determine your final certification programme lead-time.

Finally, a halal policy will need to be formulated with a corporate halal policy statement to communicating the intention (niyyah) of the company. Similar to a quality policy statement, a halal policy statement can be put on the wall in your company and shared on your corporate website.

o-base assessment

For halal certification, all products must be assessed using the halal production lines. This covers both products that will be halal-certified as well as products that will not be halal-certified but are sharing the same production lines as the halal-certified products. Material assessments require a lot of information from the supplier. Experience shows that even for multinational companies, obtaining all the necessary supplier and material information is a big challenge. Supplier information is obviously on the critical path of any halal certification programme. You can easily delay the certification process by six months if you have uncooperative suppliers. Information requests from the suppliers must be managed centrally at the highest possible level to make the supplier participate. Immediately replace suppliers of routine items, such as common ingredients you can purchase anywhere (as further explained in chapter 4), that do not cooperate with information requests. During material assessment, you will have various halal issues pop up. Our consultants use colour coding during a material assessment for each product to be assessed:

- **Green material:** allowed to be used, and supplier information is complete
- **Yellow material:** allowed to be used, but certain supplier information is missing
- **Red material:** cannot be used (prohibited material), need confirmation from HCB, halal certificate is required but the supplier does not have a halal certificate (or not the right halal certificate), etc.

When ingredients are animal-based, red item management could consume a significant amount of time and resources. Animal-based products might result in additional laboratory tests and supplier audits as requested by your HCB. Material assessments are complex and require extensive knowledge of shariah and halal standards. As a result, using an external halal expert for materials assessment will save you a lot of time and money.

Finally, the 0-base assessment also requires an assessment of your internal supply chain (receiving, production, materials handling, and distribution) to check its compliance with the halal standard requirements. Amongst others, this covers facility design, material flows, materials and equipment used, personnel, documentation, etc. The 0-base assessment requires a lot of information from both the organisation and its suppliers. A halal certification information checklist is provided in appendix 1.

HAS documentation

The setting up of a halal assurance system (HAS) requires setting up of a special department called a Halal Committee. In the bare minimum, a halal committee consists of a chairman, internal halal auditor, and representatives from key departments. Key departments are those departments that control key supply chain activities such as purchasing, production, logistics, sales, and quality assurance. For logistics companies, this could be purchasing, transport, warehousing/contract logistics, freight forwarding, and sales. The internal halal auditor typically communicates with the HCB for the application and renewal of your halal certificate. The internal halal auditor is in charge of the HAS documentation, compliance, and halal issue management. The halal committee is not necessarily a department with any full-time staff and can be a committee with employees holding other positions in the company. The halal committee regularly meets (e.g. quarterly) face-to-face or through a conference call, and whenever necessary. For companies based in predominantly Muslim countries, it is required that the chairman and internal halal auditor are Muslim. For non-Muslim countries, this would be a strong preference. The halal standard(s) followed will specify the exact requirements of a halal committee.

There are possible implications for the facility layout to ensure that halal is segregated from non-halal, there is a quarantine area for receiving, and possible halal zoning is implemented. A halal expert is able to simplify halal for your organisation and minimise changes to your operations needed. The halal standard chosen will determine the exact HAS documentation requirements. Generally, a HAS document should cover the topics as listed in table 2.1.

Implementation

For halal certification, staff must be trained on halal; not only the people in the factory or warehouse, but all members of key departments that are part of the halal committee, such as purchasing, production, logistics, marketing, and sales. To simplify halal training, it is recommended to have a halal training module incorporated in the onboarding programme for all new employees. The halal committee and the company trainers may require an annual refreshment training, providing insights into their latest HAS system and any updates on their halal standard(s) used, emerging halal requirements, and best industry practices.

The lead-time of the halal certification process, upon submission to the halal authority, differs significantly between HCBs. For some HCBs, this certification lead-time is only 2–3 months, whereas others can take up to 8–12 months. Before submission to the HCB, the halal assurance system needs to be implemented for at least three (3) months in order to create sufficient track record providing proof that you are actually operating in accordance with your HAS. The HCB will conduct both a documentation audit and physical audit of the facility for it to be halal certified.

The documentation audit assesses if the HAS and materials documentation are correct, consistent, complete, and clear (Geijn 2005). The documentation audit might be complemented by additional laboratory tests and supplier visits (e.g. if a slaughter plant is involved) upon the discretion of the auditor. The physical audit will check if the HAS has been properly implemented and ensures the compliance of its operations. Some halal authorities use online submission, whereas other halal authorities still require paper-based submission.

Summary – chapter 2: Halal assurance system (HAS)

- A halal assurance system (HAS) is an integrated management system which is developed, implemented, and maintained to manage purchasing, production/processing, materials handling, distribution, and other services in accordance with a halal standard
- A halal standard specifies the requirements of halal certification by a halal certification body (HCB). Developing the right halal certification strategy is critical in making halal simple and sustainable for your operations given your business and export goals
- Halal certification requires a halal strategy, 0-base assessment, HAS documentation, and implementation. The lead-time of a halal certification process depends on the complexity of your certification programme, support from suppliers in submitting the necessary documentation, red item management, and the efficiency of the HCB process
- As halal regulations are complex, it is recommended to recruit an external halal expert in the design and implementation of your HAS.

Reflection questions

- For which markets has halal certification value for your company (nice to have) and for which markets is halal certification mandatory (must have)?
- What is the scope of halal certification for your business: which brands, production lines, and facilities are involved? What is the best way to phase the halal certification programme in time?
- What halal certificate or combination of halal certificates are required in order to meet your business and export goals?

References

Geijn, R. van, 2005. *Natural Business Excellence*. Align Group, Bangkok.

Shah, M.S.A.A., 2017. *Halal Certification: in the Light of the Shari'ah*. Sanha Halal Associates Pakistan, Karachi,

Tieman, M., 2017. Halal Europe: A premium Halal-Tayyib brand? *Islam and Civilisational Renewal* 8(2), 260–263.

PART II

HALAL SUPPLY CHAIN MANAGEMENT

3

THE HALAL SUPPLY CHAIN

Foundation of halal supply chain management

Successful companies formulate a business strategy that determines how competitive advantage is delivered. Competitive advantage is based on the product or service and its process. The design, sourcing, production, and delivery are executed by processes in a so-called supply chain. The processes are performed by different organisations in a supply chain network. Hence, halal supply chain management is the core of halal business management.

The foundation of halal supply chain management is based on (1) direct contact with haram; (2) risk of contamination; and

(3) the perception of the Muslim consumer (figure 3.1). Direct contact with haram, better known as cross-contamination, makes a halal product non-halal and therefore not fit for consumption by Muslims. To avoid cross-contamination, primary packaging is an effective control measure. The risk of contamination is the possibility that something halal may actually become non-halal, thus moving into a state of doubt. One of the main functions of halal supply chain management is to ensure that there is no doubt (risk of contamination) in halal products. Physical segregation and communication of the halal status is an effective control measure. The perception of the Muslim consumer is shaped by the Islamic school of thought, fatwas (religious rulings), and local customs. For example, under certain Islamic schools of thought (like Shafi'i) ritual cleansing might be required before using a container. It could also mean segregation between products with a different halal certificate: segregation of a halal product from other halal products that use an 'inferior' halal standard, which is not considered halal by another Islamic country. For example, Brunei requires all meat to be hand

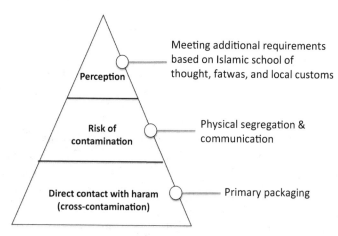

Figure 3.1 Foundation of halal supply chain management.

slaughtered and not stunned. Malaysia allows certain types of stunning. As a result, the Brunei halal authorities do not allow mixing Brunei halal-certified meat with Malaysian halal-certified meat in the same transport and storage along the supply chain.

The determinants for (1) and (2) are based on the product characteristics: cool chain versus dry chains; and bulk versus unitised. The sole determinant for (3) is based on the market requirements of the destination country. Cool chains are more sensitive than dry chains because of closed air circulation and possible moisture development on cargo. Bulk is more sensitive than unitised, as bulk has less primary packaging or none at all, exposing the product to cross-contamination with the transport vehicle and external factors (e.g. air). Unitised products have at least a primary packaging, protecting the product from cross-contamination. For non-Muslim destination countries, halal supply chains only need to comply with a minimum level of compliance based on direct contact with haram and risk of contamination. However, for predominantly Muslim destination countries, a preferred standard level is required for a halal supply chain, that also addresses the perception of the Muslim consumer (figure 3.2). As chapter 5 will show, this results in more stringent segregation requirements for predominantly Muslim destination countries as compared to non-Muslim countries.

This difference in segregation requirements has three main considerations. First of all, from a shariah (Islamic law) perspective, halal supply chains should not create unnecessary hardship for Muslims accessing halal products. Second, halal supply chains should be practical and efficient supply chains that industries in both Muslim and non-Muslim countries can follow, without endangering the halal integrity of the product. The halal integrity of an end-to-end supply chain is based on the weakest link, not the strongest link in a halal supply chain.

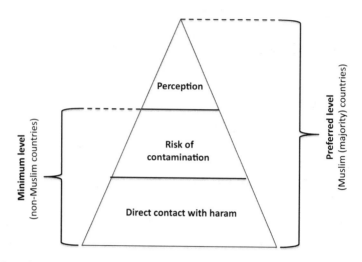

Figure 3.2 Minimum versus preferred level in halal supply chain management.

Whereas in predominantly Muslim countries, halal cargo is the norm and easy to identify and consolidate with other halal cargo; in non-Muslim countries, it is extremely difficult to identify the halal cargo status as brand owners often opt not to reveal the halal status of goods. Consolidation of halal cargo in non-Muslim countries is, therefore, an impossible puzzle to solve. Third, research shows that the majority of Muslims in non-Muslim countries are comfortable with a lower segregation level as compared to Muslims in Muslim countries (Tieman et al. 2013).

Halal supply chain model

Halal supply chains today do not have 1-to-1 relationships like a 'chain', but in fact, look more like a 'network' (figure 3.3).

THE HALAL SUPPLY CHAIN 37

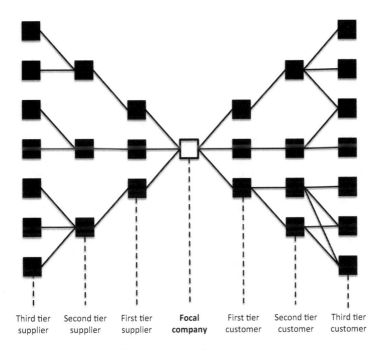

| Third tier supplier | Second tier supplier | First tier supplier | **Focal company** | First tier customer | Second tier customer | Third tier customer |

Figure 3.3 A halal supply chain network.

For example, as a producer, you have your suppliers (first-tier suppliers) and the suppliers of your suppliers (second-tier suppliers), etc. Whereas, on the other hand, as a producer you also have customers (first-tier customers) and these customers also have their own customers (second-tier customers), etc. Of course, it is good to recognize that not every supplier is of equal importance in relation to the halal integrity of a supply chain. For example, a supplier of office stationery (and their respective suppliers) does not need to be shown on a halal supply chain drawing. On the other hand, ingredients and primary packaging material suppliers need to shown on the halal supply chain diagram.

> **Halal Insight 3.1 Halal supply chain definitions**
>
> **Halal supply chain:**
> A network of connected and interdependent organisations mutually and cooperatively working together to manage, control, and improve the flow of materials and information in compliance with the general principles of shariah.
>
> **Halal supply chain management:**
> The management of a halal network with the goal of extending halal integrity from source to point of consumer purchase.
>
> **Halal logistics:**
> The process of managing the procurement, movement, storage, and handling of materials, parts, livestock, semi-finished or finished inventory of both food and non-food items, and related information and documentation flows through the organisation and the supply chain in compliance with the general principles of shariah.

While pursuing my PhD, I created the Halal Supply Chain Model (Tieman et al. 2012) for the design and management of halal supply chains. The Halal Supply Chain Model provides a strategic fit by using the formulation of a halal policy and supply chain objectives to determine the design parameters of this model. Alignment has been achieved by defining the relationship between product-market combinations and the design parameters. This Halal Supply Chain Model is shown in figure 3.4., with its components explained below.

Halal policy and supply chain objectives

Halal needs commitment from the top management level through a halal policy, which acts as a basis for the organisation

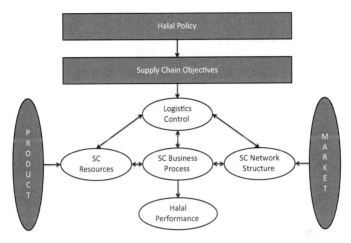

Figure 3.4 Halal supply chain model.

and its supply chain. A company will draft a halal policy statement describing its intention (niyyah). Amongst others, a halal policy statement addresses: (1) the responsibility of an organisation in protecting the halal integrity along the supply chain; (2) the scope of halal certification of the organisation; (3) the assurance to the consumer or customer (the promise); and (4) the method of assurance (control mechanism; covering aspects like halal committee, internal halal auditor, and inspection by the halal certification body). The formulated supply chain objectives (logistics and customer service objectives) direct the design parameters of halal supply chains.

Logistics control

Logistics control is the heart of the Halal Supply Chain Model, it provides the foundation for effective decision-making and management of a halal supply chain. Logistics control is the planning and control of the flow of halal goods from their source to the point of consumer purchase based on the halal requirements of the destination markets. These minimum requirements are the logistics design parameter that will be shared throughout the supply chain network for a particular product-market combination.

Supply chain resources

Supply chain resources define the organisation and information management. For a halal-certified organisation, as described in chapter 2, a halal committee is required. The halal committee is responsible for the compliance of the halal supply chain to one or multiple halal standards. People in the organisation, as well as the supply chain partners, must be trained on halal.

Information management, identifying and communicating the halal status of cargo using a 'Halal Supply Chain' code, has been argued to be one of the critical success factors for effective halal supply chains. As I always say, your segregation is as good as your communication. The minimum requirement for tracking and tracing is having tier 1 customers and suppliers as the width of traceability; and the chain of custody as the depth of traceability.

Supply chain network structure

The reality of supply chain structures is that only a fraction of supply chain partners are halal-certified (maybe 5%). Some supply chain partners maintain halal SOPs (maybe 15%), whereas most of supply chain partners (maybe 80%) have no halal SOPs at all (figure 3.5). Halal supply chains are therefore vulnerable supply chains. Supply chain configurations can be a source of various risks: partner-related risks as well as internal organisational risks, and process-related risks. To preserve the integrity of halal supply chains, it is therefore crucial that the parties involved in a halal supply chain are halal-certified (preferred) or comply with the

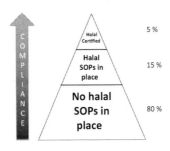

Figure 3.5 Supply chain partner classification.

halal supply chain requirements as set by your organisation. Even though a supply chain partner is halal-certified, it is necessary to include in detail the relevant halal control points and control measures in a contract.

The halal integrity of a supply chain network is founded on halal supply chain requirements that are incorporated in contract clauses with your key supply chain partners. Key supply chain partners are those supply chain partners that are part of the so-called managed process links: supply chain links that are most critical for maintaining halal integrity.

As the supply chain halal integrity is a function of the integrity of your supply chain links, the choice of supply chain partners should receive top priority in the design of supply chain network structures. Simple supply chain structures are preferred and there is a need for vertical and horizontal collaboration in halal supply chains. These two forms of collaboration will be discussed in more detail later in this chapter.

Supply chain business processes

For halal supply chains, the supply chain business processes 'customer order fulfilment', 'manufacturing flow management', and 'purchasing' are of particular importance. First, the customer order fulfilment process carries the segregation requirements of the customer (based on the destination market) throughout the supply chain. Second, manufacturing flow management is the physical handling of the halal product throughout the supply chain, for which halal control measures must be formulated to extend the halal integrity from the source to the point of consumer purchase. This process also covers logistics and will be discussed at length in chapter 5. Third, purchasing is critical in a halal supply chain, for its role in defining and managing the upstream supply chain network structure through supplier management and the purchasing process. For more details on purchasing, please refer to chapter 4.

Halal performance

To measure the performance of halal supply chains, first, it is of utmost importance to measure the effectiveness perspective of a supply chain. This would address three key aspects namely halal reputation, process quality, and waste. Halal reputation is measured through the halal reputation index and licence to operate rating, which is discussed in chapter 10. Process quality addresses areas such as the trustworthiness of a brand and includes consumer complaints received regarding the halal status of a product. Waste addresses the physical waste in a supply chain, including the carbon footprint and resources used. It is good to realise that waste occurs both within the supply chain as well as by the end-consumer.

Second, halal supply chains should also be efficient in order to avoid an escalation of halal (food) prices. This would particularly affect Muslim consumers living in non-Muslim countries, which would create hardship for them in sourcing their daily needs. Efficiency is first of all measured by supply chain costs. For supply chains that use dedicated halal logistics assets, another suitable indicator of efficiency is the utilisation of these halal warehouse facilities and transportation.

Third, halal supply chains should be robust by design in order to better protect the halal integrity of halal products along the supply chain under different circumstances. Important strategies comprise the development of a strong alliance network, lead-time reductions, and vertical and horizontal collaboration. The robustness of a halal supply chain should first of all result in few halal-related rejections. Second, a halal supply chain should have sufficient access to halal warehouse facilties and halal transportion when required according to its halal supply chain design principles.

Design principles for predominantly Muslim and non-Muslim countries

For non-Muslim countries, a halal supply chain is based on the minimum level: direct contact with haram and risk of contamination. For predominantly Muslim countries, this is based on the preferred level: direct contact with haram, risk of contamination, and the perception of the Muslim consumer. This has been described in figure 3.2. These differences translate into differences in the halal control points and control measures and will be discussed in chapter 5. Here, I propose dedicated warehouses and designated transport for predominantly Muslim countries and controlled segregation for non-Muslim countries based on the product characteristics.

Design principles for different product characteristics

Bulk cargo does not allow the mixing of halal and non-halal products in any circumstance. A cool chain (chilled or frozen) environment is more sensitive to contamination than a dry (ambient) environment. The result is no mixing of halal with severe najis (ritually unclean) unitised products in the same cold room and refrigerated transport unit for non-Muslim countries. There should absolutely be no mixing of halal with non-halal products on one pallet or load carrier. For predominantly Muslim countries halal and non-halal products are completely segregated at all times in storage and transport regardless of the product characteristics. This will be discussed in more detail in chapter 5. The result of the product-market design principles is shown in figure 3.6.

Synergy in halal supply chains

As managing a halal supply chain network is a complex task, there is big potential for improving the performance of halal supply chains through collaboration. Halal synergy can be achieved with both vertical and horizontal collaboration. In vertical collaboration, you cooperate with suppliers, service providers, and customers within your own supply chain network. Whereas in horizontal collaboration, you join forces with other supply chains when engaging with competitors and

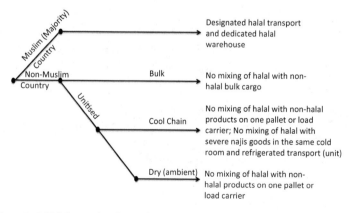

Figure 3.6 Halal supply chain design principles.

non-competitors. Horizontal collaboration as an instrument has rarely been applied by the halal industry, for reasons of confidentiality and resistance to working with competitors, leaving a lot of potential synergy advantages unexplored.

Vertical collaboration (figure 3.7) of halal supply chains can be achieved through halal clusters and halal supply chain orchestrators. Halal clusters are the geographical clustering of halal production chains (halal food, cosmetics, pharmaceuticals, etc.). Clusters provide evident logistical advantages (e.g. shorter transport times); optimal use of by-products, including waste and energy; increased capacity for cluster participants and innovation growth; and stimulate new business formation that supports innovation, and expands the halal cluster. Chapter 6 will discuss halal clusters in more detail.

A halal supply chain orchestrator assists in managing global halal supply chains according to the specification of the destination market and ensures that the integrity is maintained throughout the

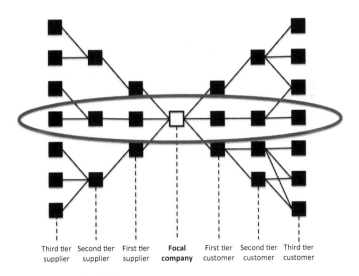

Figure 3.7 Vertical collaboration.

halal supply chain network. This orchestrator makes use of common halal distribution centres in key gateways, such as consolidation in transport and the use of innovative logistics concepts (like a halal cargo box). This role can be fulfilled by a third-party or fourth-party logistics service provider: an integrator that assembles the resources, planning capabilities, and technology of its own organisation and other organisations to design, build, and run comprehensive halal supply chain solutions.

Vertical collaboration allows for:

- **Effective halal supply chain assurance:** strict reference to one international halal logistics standard and consistent communication of the halal status ('halal supply chain' code) throughout the supply chain;
- **Standardisation of halal assets in a supply chain:** from source to the point of consumer purchase; and
- **Supply chain optimisation:** sharing demand data through the supply chain, reducing inventories, and better transport planning.

Horizontal collaboration provides massive business benefits for manufacturers, retailers, and restaurant chains. Horizontal collaboration (figure 3.8) can be facilitated through direct collaboration between different companies, or through an intermediary such as a third-party logistics service provider. Direct collaboration among different companies can be achieved through four possible collaboration methods.

First, there could be a dominant industry player, where smaller companies could use the halal assets or supplier contract (for example a contract with a transporter or warehouse operator) of the dominant player in the facilitation of the halal transport and/or warehousing requirements of the other players. The dominant player has developed the halal assets or supplier

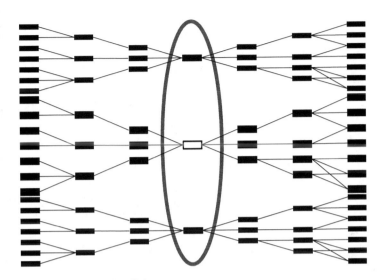

Figure 3.8 Horizontal collaboration.

contract based on his specifications only, whereas the others are using his assets or contract. It is a low-cost method, but might lead to objections from the supplier.

A second possibility is that transport is facilitated by company A, warehousing facilitated by company B, and halal containers by company C. The choice between which company will be used to facilitate which activity is based on the expertise, resources, or volume.

The third way is through a collaboration between companies in the same industry on a project basis. For example, it could be ideal to facilitate a joint supply from one country to the Kingdom of Saudi Arabia to meet the food, cosmetics, and medical requirements during the Hajj season. Another application could be a temporary collaboration between companies in the supply of humanitarian aid during a crisis situation. This will require an integrated supply chain management approach to effectively coordinate inter-agency performance, eliminate redundancies, and maximise efficiencies.

The fourth method is a continuous and intensive collaboration between companies where many activities are done jointly together. This could be applicable when companies are based in the same halal cluster to facilitate the sourcing of halal raw materials (as well as other products and services) and handling the distribution of halal goods. An intermediary is able to consolidate the flows of halal goods for different companies that need domestic road transport, cross border transport, air shipments, sea shipments, warehousing, and value-added logistics (like repacking and customisation to certain Muslim markets). Here, various companies can make use of the expertise in the global network and the ability to consolidate halal flows by this intermediary for a more effective and efficient management of the various halal logistics requirements according to the destination market.

Consolidation is one of the most important services offered by third-party logistics service providers, where they could deliver collaborative advantages to the halal industry.

Horizontal collaboration allows for:

- **Sharing of information:** 'halal supply chain' code, best practices in halal supply chain and value chain, and halal specifications [machine slaughter: yes/no; stunning: yes/no]
- **Pooling of resources:** outsourcing to a common (halal certified or compliant) third party logistics service provider, sharing halal assets (for example a halal warehouse and designated halal transport); and
- **Bundling of halal volumes:** reducing transport costs, improved segregation conditions.

Halal blockchains

Most halal supply chains have inherent flaws namely in traceability (ability to verify the halal status by the consumer) and facilitating product recalls; transport and storage compliance downstream the supply chain in accordance with halal requirements of the destination market; end-to-end chain integrity (unbroken chain): from source to the point of consumer purchase; different halal systems and interpretations of different markets; and lack of integration of information technology.

These problems require a radically different approach to better organise halal supply chains. Halal blockchains have the potential for solving these halal supply chain problems. Blockchain technology could provide halal trust of products and their supply chains, and create halal synergy advantages.

Halal blockchains execute supply chains based on the halal requirements of the destination market, which are determined by the Islamic school of thought, fatwas (religious rulings), and local customs. Halal blockchains could be relevant for both Muslim and non-Muslim countries. Halal certification requirements of the destination market and mutual recognition are critical design principles for halal blockchains. Supply chain participants are automatically aligned and instructed on process compliance based on the specific product-market supply chain scenarios. Data security of halal blockchains are essential to protect confidential information and minimise the chance and impact of cyber-attacks. Figure 3.9 shows the halal blockchain concept.

Smart contracts are pre-agreed autonomous programmes that define supply chain relationships as well as automatic actions. In the case of halal issues, the blockchain system triggers automatic action based on the smart contract's set terms.

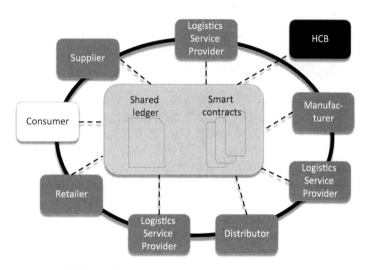

Figure 3.9 Halal blockchain.

Key smart contracts for a halal blockchain are:

- **Supply chain execution:** segregation and communication (coding on freight document, cargo labels, and IT system) requirements for a product-market scenario;
- **Halal issue management:** identification and diagnosis of a halal issue based on the blockchain and communicating blockchain information to the relevant halal certification body (HCB) for a decision on the halal status (halal or haram)
- **Product recalls:** identify and isolate an affected production batch, inform the supply chain, take the affected goods out of the trade, and inform the consumer (in case of a public recall).

Automatic actions reduce lead-times in solving halal issues. Speed reduces sales and corporate reputation damages that are triggered by a halal issue.

Performance measurement of halal supply chains and their participants is critical to ensure high-performance supply chains. First, this requires a classification of halal blockchain participants in terms of halal compliance as shown in figure 3.5. Second, the actual halal performance must be tracked in the areas of efficiency, effectiveness, and robustness.

Manufacturers, brand owners, and retailers benefit from halal blockchains, particularly through the transparency of supply chain, synergy advantages through vertical and horizontal collaboration, standardisation of halal assets, and more effective risk and reputation management. Logistics service providers and distributors benefit from halal blockchains, particularly through long-term customer relations, higher utilisation of halal assets, consolidation of halal cargo, value-added logistics and services, digitalisation of paper flows, and more efficient payment settlement. Halal certification bodies benefit from halal blockchains, particularly through easy auditing of halal supply chains, and by providing faster support for industries in case of a halal issue and crisis. In summary, blockchain technology is a promising technology that can help control complex halal supply chain networks, and thus optimises its performance.

Summary – chapter 3: Halal supply chain

- The foundation of halal supply chain management is based on direct contact with haram, risk of contamination, and the perception of the Muslim consumer. The minimum level, which is applicable in non-Muslim countries, is based on direct contact with haram and risk of contamination only. The preferred level, which is applicable in predominantly Muslim countries, addresses all three components: direct contact with haram, risk of contamination, and the perception of the Muslim consumer

- The Halal Supply Chain Model provides a management model for the design and management of halal supply chains. Product characteristics and market requirements determine the design criteria of halal supply chain networks
- As managing a halal supply chain network is a complex task, there is significant potential in the improvement of the performance of halal supply chains through collaboration. Halal synergy can be achieved with both vertical and horizontal collaboration
- Blockchain technology, the combination of the distributed ledger technology with smart contracts, has the potential for better control in high-performance halal supply chain networks

Reflection questions

- What are your product characteristics and market requirements?
- What does your supply chain structure look like?
- How can you improve synergy advantages through collaboration within your supply chain network (vertical collaboration) and with other supply chain networks (horizontal collaboration)?

References

Tieman, M., van der Vorst, J. G., Ghazali, M. C., 2012. Principles in halal supply chain management. Journal of Islamic Marketing 3 (3), 217–243. https://doi.org/10.1108/17590831211259727.

Tieman, M., Ghazali, M. C., Van Der Vorst, J. G., 2013. Consumer perception on halal meat logistics. British Food Journal 115 (8), 1112–1129. https://doi.org/10.1108/BFJ-10/2011-0265.

4

HALAL PURCHASING

Halal procurement maturity

Purchasing is the professional buying done by organisations. Purchasing defines the buyer-supplier relationship. Since most companies today spend more than half of their sales turnover on purchasing products, services, and works, purchasing has become a key business management function.

Purchasing is a critical halal business management function for the following reasons:

- Purchasing guarantees all products and services sourced are halal and compliant with halal certification requirements

- Purchasing builds, maintains, and controls a sustainable supplier base with the appropriate and valid halal certificates
- Purchasing ensures all supply chain partners contracted by the company are halal compliant, which is enforced through contractual agreement and supplier audits
- Purchasing screens halal purchase market developments, providing intelligence on the supply risk for commodity categories identified

Purchasing will need to maintain excellent relationships with other departments, such as research and development, production, logistics, and marketing and sales. Early involvement of purchasing is mission-critical for effective halal purchasing.

Halal has clear implications for the purchasing function. The halal industry traditionally has been addressing halal at the 'specification stage' only: make sure that ingredients A, B, and C have a halal certificate from HCB X or a halal certificate recognised by this HCB. This is a myopic view of halal purchasing, which will result in an unstable halal purchasing and halal assurance system (HAS) for any halal-certified organisation.

The halal procurement maturity model in Table 4.1 provides guidance in establishing a solid halal purchasing function. The proposed halal procurement maturity model recognises three stages: (1) viewing halal compliance as an opportunity; (2) making supply chains halal; and (3) making value chains halal.

At the first stage, the primary task is to get the so-called 'house in order'. Amongst others, this covers halal certification of the organisation, establishing a halal committee, and defining and communicating their halal policy. As a competitive advantage, it is important to create awareness in the organisation of the value of halal compliance through in-house training and internal awareness campaigns. For this step, purchasing includes

Table 4.1 Halal procurement maturity model

	Stage 1 Viewing halal compliance as an opportunity	Stage 2 Making supply chains halal	Stage 3 Making value chains halal
Challenge:	To ensure that pro-active halal compliance provides a competitive advantage for the company	To support a transition to a halal supply chain	To support a transition to a halal value chain
Competencies:	Products of the company are halal-certified; Halal Committee is established; Halal Policy is defined	A halal purchasing team is established; The skills to audit suppliers; The ability to generate real support for halal supply chains; The ability to redesign halal supply chains	Expertise in Islamic banking and financing; The ability to redesign products that are less animal-based and more sustainable
Purchasing opportunities:	Assessing halal compliance of supplier base; Using compliance to induce supply chain partners to obtain halal certification	Audit high-risk suppliers to ensure that their operations comply with your halal standard(s); Harmonisation of halal standards used in the supply chain; Implement improvements in the procurement strategy and purchasing processes	Review purchasing contracts; Replace animal-based ingredients with plant-based ingredients; ensuring the environmental sustainability of suppliers

assessing the current halal compliance of all suppliers in terms of halal certification for those commodity categories where halal is important, such as ingredients, primary packaging, logistics, food processing equipment, MRO (maintenance, repair and operations), etc. A practical tool for this is the Halal Compliance Matrix as suggested in Figure 4.1.

The Halal Compliance Matrix has two axes: one for the halal commodity categories and one for halal compliance. The commodity category axis shows the total number of suppliers involved in the halal commodity categories, whereas the halal compliance axis represents the percentage of suppliers in the commodity category that are actually halal certified. The order of the commodity categories on the vertical axis is determined by the halal compliance scores. The total halal compliance of the supplier base is equal to the area: I/(area I+ areas II). The matrix provides a quick overview of the biggest halal compliance issues. In the sourcing of animal-based ingredients, special attention is paid to the specification of halal, namely machine slaughtered [yes/no] and stunning [yes/no], the requirements of which both depend on the halal certification of the factory and the

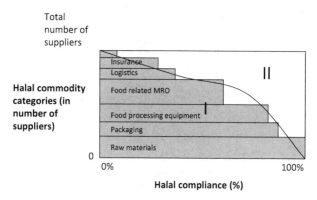

Figure 4.1 Halal compliance matrix.

requirements of the destination market (which may be more stringent).

For the second stage, a so-called halal purchasing team is established. Primarily, this cross-functional team is tasked with identifying, selecting, and managing suppliers for halal relevant product groups. High-risk suppliers, such as suppliers of animal-based products or suppliers based in a non-Muslim country, require a more stringent auditing process compared to other suppliers. The second important function of the halal purchasing team is to harmonise halal standards of suppliers, through an active dialogue with the domestic halal authority and their suppliers. Thirdly, the halal purchasing team is responsible for identifying and implementing any changes required in the procurement strategy and purchasing processes of the company.

Then at the third stage, the halal purchasing team becomes the key driver in reviewing contracts to meet shariah requirements. Islam promotes genuine trade and business transactions. It prohibits interest, excessive ambiguity, and gambling (speculation) (ISRA 2011). This should be carefully reviewed in purchasing contracts. This could also be a factor in future contracts for the purchase of agriculture commodities and oil and gas. Islamic banking products and insurance (*takaful*), where possible, are used at this stage. Second, the halal purchasing team is an important partner in replacing animal-based ingredients with plant-based ingredients. Third, the halal purchasing team, in achieving excellence with its supplier base, is responsible for ensuring the environmental sustainability of its suppliers.

The halal purchasing function of an organisation, shown in Figure 4.2, consists of three building blocks: halal policy, procurement strategy, and purchasing process. The halal policy, as defined by the management of the company, directs both the

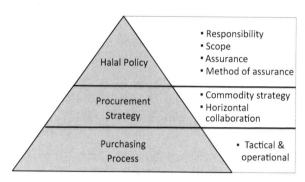

Figure 4.2 Halal purchasing function.

procurement strategy and purchasing process. The following sections provide practical guidelines and tools for a halal procurement strategy and halal purchasing process.

Halal procurement strategy

In the groundbreaking article 'Purchasing must become supply management' published in the Harvard Business Review of 1983, Peter Kraljic shares the foundation of procurement strategy (Kraljic 1983). His procurement concepts are still the leading theory for procurement strategy as we know it today.

In his work, the procurement strategy for a commodity category is based on the importance of purchasing and supply risk. The importance of purchasing for a commodity category is often measured as the cost of purchasing a commodity category over a 12-month period. Supply risk for a commodity category is measured against criteria such as the number of potential suppliers, availability of supply, competitive structure in supply markets, etc. This results in a matrix with four quadrants for a distinctive commodity category procurement strategy:

- **Routine product**: large choice of suppliers with similar products; low importance of purchase. Strategy: Reduce the number of suppliers and reduce internal administrative costs
- **Leverage product**: large choice of suppliers with similar products; high importance of the purchase. Strategy: Exploit power position for the advantage of the buying company, and medium-term contracts
- **Strategic product**: limited choice of suppliers; high importance of purchase. Strategy: Long-term (win-win) supply relationship, contingency planning, and vendor control
- **Bottleneck product**: limited choice of suppliers; low importance of purchase. Strategy: Volume insurance (at cost premium if necessary), control of vendors, and backup plans

The implication of halal for the conventional commodity category allocation on the Kraljic Portfolio Matrix has two possible effects. First, halal has an impact on the importance of purchasing for producers of halal sensitive products, namely: 'Is the product animal-based?' [yes/no]. Examples of animal-based products are raw meat, processed meat, ingredients/additives derived from animals (like gelatine), and processed products that contain these items. If the product is animal-based it moves a traditional routine product to leverage or a bottleneck product to strategic.

Second, halal has an impact on the supply risk based on the country of the supplier: 'Is the supply chain partner based in a non-Muslim country?' [yes/no]. Partners in non-Muslim countries that offer halal products and services have invested in halal certification/compliance, are specialised, and are often not well controlled and supported by its government in terms of its halal

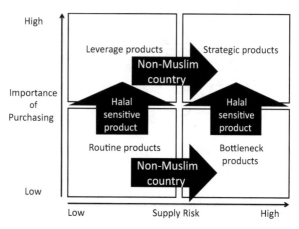

Figure 4.3 The Kraljic Portfolio Matrix.

regulations. This requires a more intensive relationship with these suppliers, which moves a traditional routine product to bottleneck or a leverage product to strategic for non-Muslim countries. The implication of halal on the Kraljic Portfolio Matrix is summarised in Figure 4.3.

When combining the effect of halal sensitivity and country forces on the Kraljic Portfolio Matrix (Figure 4.4), it could move a simple animal-based additive traditionally classified as routine product to a strategic product, which has major consequences for the procurement strategy and supplier management. A fruit concentrate sourced from Germany now becomes a bottleneck product (instead of a routine product). Meat sourced from Brazil is no longer a leverage product, but a strategic product instead. As can be deduced from the strategies for each quadrant as described by Kraljic (1983), halal leads to stronger partnerships with suppliers and adopting various strategies to secure continuity of supply.

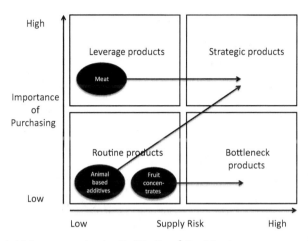

Figure 4.4 Movements in the Kraljic Portfolio Matrix.

Horizontal collaboration

The idea of collaboration among purchasing organisations is increasingly being explored by industries in search of better prices, better service levels, and reducing supply risks. In horizontal collaboration in purchasing you cooperate with other purchasing organisations (competitors and/or non-competitors), where you can create synergy advantages. Synergy advantages in particular are targeted in terms of cost reductions (important for leverage products) and reduction of supply risks (important for bottleneck products). Horizontal collaboration in the purchasing of leverage products could allow for better contracts (price, service level, and other conditions) and a sustainable supply (e.g. animal-based ingredients and additives). Horizontal collaboration in purchasing is also essential for bottleneck products to reduce supply risk. This could be relevant for example for non-animal-based ingredients and additives sourced from non-Muslim countries,

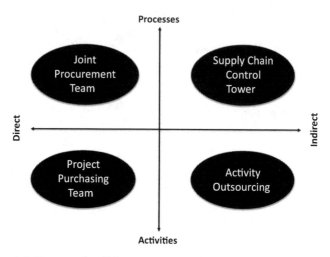

Figure 4.5 Horizontal collaboration in purchasing.

and sourcing of cool chain transport and warehousing solutions. Horizontal collaboration allows harvesting synergy advantages that are now often left on the table. Figure 4.5 classifies four different horizontal collaboration models in halal purchasing based on (1) direct versus indirect collaboration; and (2) activity versus process collaboration. What are the possible horizontal collaboration models available to industries?

Joint procurement team:

- **Franchise formula or cooperative**: under one corporate brand (e.g. Spar Retail Formula, McDonald's restaurant chain) leveraging purchasing volume, asset control, inventory sharing, warehousing and transport sharing, and standardisation of halal assurance system and certification
- **Direct collaboration between different (and competing) organisations**: leveraging purchasing volume, inventory sharing, and harmonisation of halal standards

Project purchasing team:

- **Crisis management**: in case of a lockdown situation (like during the corona crisis of 2020), humanitarian aid, or during a natural disaster, certain activities such as transport and warehousing is combined, to ensure continuity of supply and deliveries
- **Hajj/Umrah supplies**: harmonisation of halal standards for supplies to Hajj/Umrah pilgrims in Mecca and Medina (Kingdom of Saudi Arabia), as well as combining transport and warehousing needs

Activity outsourcing:

- Sourcing of halal ingredients through a specialised **marketplace** (e.g. the e-commerce platform OneAgrix)
- Halal transport, warehouse, value-added logistics outsourcing to a halal-certified third-party **logistics service provider** (3PL) (e.g. DB Schenker)
- Outsourcing of product packaging or bottling to a halal-certified **packaging/bottling company**

Supply Chain Control Tower:

- **Operational control tower** provided by non-asset based fourth-party logistics service providers (4PL), supporting purchase order planning, supply chain visibility, and exception management

The preference for one or a combination of horizontal collaboration models depends on several factors, such as: synergy potential, halal maturity of an organisation (table 1.1), halal procurement maturity (table 4.1), business culture, size of an organisation (SME, large, multinational), and location in the halal cluster (chapter 6).

Halal purchasing process

For the purchasing process, the classification of Weele (2002) is often used. According to Weele (2002), the purchasing process consists of six steps: (1) determine specifications; (2) select supplier; (3) contracting; (4) ordering; (5) expediting and evaluation; and (6) follow-up and evaluation. The first three steps are called tactical purchasing. This is the traditional responsibility of the purchasing department, wherein direct collaboration with the internal customer, the product, service, or work specifications are clearly formulated, suppliers are searched for and selected; and the supplier is then contracted. The last three steps are called operational purchasing, where the products, services, or works are ordered and delivered to the company. Here the internal customer normally plays a more dominant role; whereas purchasing and finance provide a supporting administrative function. Now the question is: 'How does halal impact these six purchasing process steps?' Figure 4.6 presents an overview.

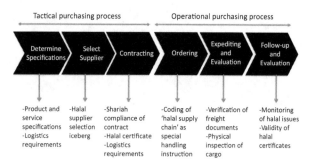

Figure 4.6 The Van Weele Purchasing Process.

Determine specifications

Amongst others, a purchase order specification should clearly address:

- Halal certificate(s) required for products (e.g. ingredients, additives, primary packing materials) and services (e.g. packing/bottling, logistics, clean(s)ing services, insurance) purchased
- Storage, transport, and handling requirements for the product purchased according to a local and/or international halal (logistics) standard

Select supplier

As discussed in chapter 3, supplier selection is pivotal for implementing an effective, efficient, and robust halal supply chain. This justifies a particular effort for this purchasing process step. Conventional supplier selection criteria address aspects such as price/cost competitiveness, product quality, delivery performance, financial condition, technical competence, management capabilities, and innovation (Monczka et al. 2005). With the purchase of halal products and services, additional factors must be covered in supplier selection beyond the physical halal products and its ingredients: not only the *what* (physical product) but also the *how* (the process) (Al-Qaradawi 2007, Wilson and Liu 2010). Figure 4.7 presents these halal supplier selection criteria.

First, the physical halal product and its components/ingredients should be halal. This can be complex as you need to look into areas such as the halal slaughtering requirements, use of animal-based enzymes, allowed parts of the animal to be used for human consumption, and permitted alcohol percentage in ingredients. Second, does the supplier have a halal policy? This shows the halal

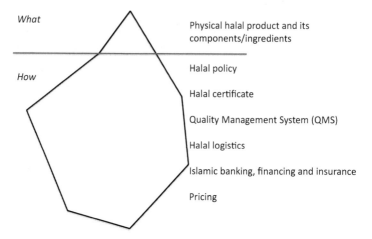

Figure 4.7 Halal supplier selection iceberg.

commitment of the organisation. Third, does the company have a halal certificate from a trusted halal certification body (HCB)? This provides assurance that the ingredients/components and operations process were verified by an independent HCB to meet shariah requirements. Fourth, does the product meet high product quality and health and safety standards? As discussed in chapter 2, the quality management system (QMS) is the foundation of the Halal Assurance System (HAS). Without a solid QMS, the HAS might not be sustainable. Fifth, is halal compliance addressed in logistics (transport and storage) by the supplier? Lack of halal compliance in transport and storage endangers the halal integrity of the entire supply chain. Sixth, in the execution of the contract, is shariah compliance in banking, finance, and insurance addressed by the supplier? Shariah prohibits interest, excessive ambiguity, and gambling (speculation), which has implications for the banking, financing, and insurance (ISRA 2011). Finally, is the pricing fair and free from interest, excessive ambiguity, and speculation?

It could be argued that for suppliers in predominantly Muslim countries all components of the Halal Supplier Selection Iceberg are important, whereas for non-Muslim countries less stringent practices are allowed in areas such as halal policy, logistics, Islamic banking-finance-insurance, and pricing.

Contracting

The interest and benefits of both parties need to be protected in halal compliant contracts. This requires at least the following three checks:

- In the contract, is there a clause for interest, excessive ambiguity, and speculation?
- Does the contract refer to the required halal certificate(s) and the validity of the halal certificate(s)?
- In terms of delivery, is there a reference to a halal (logistics) standard? Does the contract specify the halal control points and control measures in transport and storage (see chapter 5)?

Ordering

Upon ordering, a purchase order is placed with the supplier against contract conditions. It is important to have a 'halal supply chain' coded as special handling instruction (see chapter 5). This allows the logistics players and other supply chain parties involved (like customs and other inspection authorities) to identify the halal status of a shipment and handle halal cargo in accordance with halal standards and SOPs. This prevents the halal supply chain integrity from being immediately broken at each hand-off in the supply chain.

Expediting and evaluation

Upon receiving the goods at the site, freight documents are first verified to avoid bringing in haram products that may contaminate your halal facility. When the freight documents are in order, only then is the cargo physically inspected to ensure that the right products, with the right halal certificates, are in the right condition. If the packaging is damaged, the halal status could be affected. This needs to be assessed through inspection and clarification in a designated quarantine area.

Follow-up and evaluation

The follow-up and evaluation covers settling claims, keeping supplier files up-to-date, and supplier rating. In particular, attention is paid to the monitoring of halal issues with deliveries from the supplier, and the validity of halal certificates. The validity of the halal certificate is based on the expiry date of the halal certificate as well as the recognition of the halal certification body that issued the halal certificate to the supplier. For effective supplier management and sustainability of the halal assurance system (HAS), there are advantages when the supplier monitoring is automated to issue early warnings to purchasing as well as to your supplier.

Summary – chapter 4: Halal purchasing

- Purchasing is a critical halal business management function in developing a sustainable Halal Assurance System (HAS). Halal requirements have implications for both the procurement strategy and purchasing process
- Halal leads to stronger partnerships with suppliers (strategic and leverage products) and adopting various strategies to secure continuity of supply (bottleneck products)

- Horizontal collaboration is an important halal procurement strategy, which differentiates four possible models: joint procurement team, project purchasing team, activity outsourcing, and supply chain control tower
- Halal has implications for both the tactical and operational purchasing process, where automation of supplier monitoring has evident advantages

Reflection questions

- What is my current halal procurement maturity, where should I still do more work, and how do I elevate my purchasing organisation to the next level?
- Are my procurement strategies and my purchasing processes optimised for the purchase of halal products and services?
- What horizontal collaboration models can I explore for which commodity categories?

References

Al-Qaradawi, Y., 2007. The Lawful and the Prohibited in Islam. Islamic Book Trust, Petaling Jaya.

ISRA., 2011. Islamic Financial System: Principles & Operations. International Shiri'ah Research Academy for Islamic Finance, Kuala Lumpur.

Kraljic, P. (1983). Purchasing must become supply management. Harvard Business Review. September/October. 61(5), 109–117.

Monczka, R., Trent, R., Handfield, R., 2005. Purchasing and Supply Chain Management, Third ed. Thompson, London.

Weele, J. van, 2002. Purchasing and Supply Chain Management: Analysis, Planning and Practice, Third ed. Thomson, London.

Wilson, J. A. J., Liu, J., 2010. Shaping the halal into a brand. Journal of Islamic Marketing 1 (2), 107–123. https://doi.org/10.1108/17590831011055851.

5

HALAL LOGISTICS AND RETAILING

The halal logistics service provider

Today, most companies outsource their logistics to a logistics service provider. The logistics service provider has become a key supply chain partner in extending halal integrity from the source to the point of consumer purchase. Although logistics activities and processes can be outsourced, the responsibility of the halal integrity still lies with the brand owner. Failure to control the integrity of a halal supply chain by the brand owner will result in halal issues and potentially losing your licence to operate and your halal certificate. Contracting a halal-certified logistics service provider has advantages as it already has a halal assurance system in place. This provides assurance that there are SOPs in the segregation of halal from non-halal in transport and storage, but also that the halal status is identified and communicated throughout the supply chain.

Logistics service providers are experts in managing complex supply chain networks. They have specialised supply chain management systems, control assets, and have logistics partners in all corners of the world. Even though a logistics service provider is halal-certified, it is still essential for the brand owner to specify the level of segregation, communication specifications, and other service requirements (such as ritual cleansing). As there are many halal certificates being used in the logistics industry, with few prescriptive halal logistics standards available, there is very little harmonisation of halal control points and control measures in logistics. Hence, the contract with your logistics service provider, which specifies the halal control points and control measures in logistics, still remains the basis of the halal supply chain process and halal performance of your logistics service provider.

As the halal industry is moving from a product approach towards a halal supply chain approach, there is an evident demand for halal logistics services to support local, regional, and global halal supply chains. Figure 5.1 shows a classification of halal logistics service providers based on two dimensions: (1) supply chain activities versus supply chain processes; and (2) asset-heavy versus non-asset based.

Asset-heavy supply chain activities are the halal warehouse, halal transport, and halal compliant (sea/air/inland) terminals. These organisations have a halal assurance system in place to protect the halal integrity of cargo when using their assets. They can have dedicated halal assets (halal only warehouse or transport), designated halal assets in space and time (halal warehouse zone, halal container shipment from Jakarta to Rotterdam), or

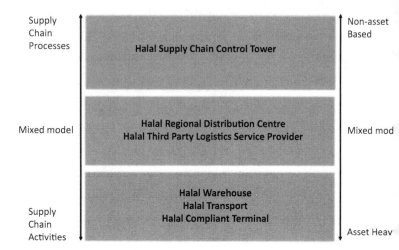

Figure 5.1 Classification of halal logistics service providers.

halal compliant (sea/air/inland) terminals where halal is properly segregated during the terminal process. In many countries, there are halal-certified warehouse operators and transporters. Over the years, there have been various halal seaport initiatives in the world, for example in the Netherlands, Belgium, Spain, Malaysia, and Indonesia. With regard to airports, there are some air cargo handlers offering halal air cargo handling services such as in Malaysia for instance.

The Halal Regional Distribution Centre (HRDC) facilitates regional and global halal sourcing and distribution, as well as value-added logistics activities such as repacking, customisation, and light processing, leveraging the halal brand of a country. Leveraging the country's halal brand is possible by conducting light processing or repacking operations in a country which has a strong halal reputation (e.g. 'Made in Saudi Arabia' or 'Packed in Saudi Arabia') as compared to conducting these activities in a country with a poor halal reputation or no halal regulations in place (e.g. 'Made in Europe' or 'Packed in Europe').

The halal third-party logistics service provider (3PL) is a logistics service provider offering outsourced warehousing, transport, and supply chain management. The 3PL has regional or global operations with a quality management system and a halal assurance system that is standardised over the various countries the 3PL is operational. This ensures that the halal integrity is kept intact for their clients' regional and global supply chains. For companies with regional and global operations, engaging a halal-certified 3PL has evident advantages from a halal risk management point of view. Although initially championed by local logistics services providers, since the past years, various multinational 3PLs have obtained a halal certificate, such as DB Schenker, DHL, Nichirei Corporation, and Nippon Express.

The Halal Supply Chain Control Tower is a non-asset based fourth-party logistics service provider (4PL), providing real-time order planning, supply chain visibility, and exception management. The control tower focuses on the command and control of multi-enterprise halal supply chain networks optimising across halal supply chain networks and ensuring end-to-end halal integrity. Although non-asset based, the control tower is IT heavy, supported by advanced supply chain management systems.

Logistics service providers can opt to get halal certified according to a local halal standard or an international halal logistics/supply chain standard. The question is: what halal standard or combination of halal standards would be optimal for a logistics service provider? For companies mainly operating within a country, such as a warehouse facility and local transporter/trucker, a local halal (logistics) standard would be sufficient. For companies doing both local and international logistics, there are advantages to have both certificates, where the international certificate acts as the halal assurance system backbone for regional or global operations. This ensures consistency in your regional or global operations.

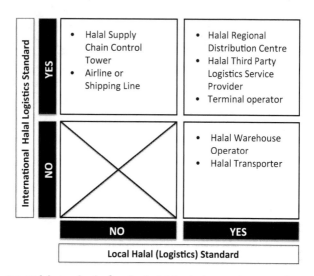

Figure 5.2 Halal standards for the halal logistics service provider.

For purely international operations, such as airlines and shipping lines, the international halal logistics standard could be sufficient. Figure 5.2 summarises the different halal certification scenarios for halal logistics service providers.

Halal certification will soon move from an order winner ('halal certification will allow me to win more business') to a market qualifier ('halal certification is a minimum requirement for doing business') in Islamic countries. For logistics service providers halal certification will be part of your licence to operate in Muslim-majority countries for most commodities.

Halal warehouse

A halal warehouse is a dedicated space for the storage and handling of goods and materials that are in compliance with shariah. For cargo destined to predominantly Muslim countries, a halal warehouse needs to be a dedicated halal warehouse facility (preferred level), whereas, for cargo destined to non-Muslim countries, a halal warehouse can be limited to a halal zone within a general warehouse (minimum level). Although a dedicated halal warehouse facility is easier to manage than a halal zone, this is not always economical in non-Muslim countries.

Figure 5.3 shows the standard warehouse processes. For a dedicated halal warehouse, the halal control points are limited to receiving, putaway, and shipping processes only. For a non-dedicated halal warehouse, on the other hand, halal control points are in all warehouse processes: receiving, putaway, storage, value-added logistics (VAL), cross-docking, order picking, and shipping. Table 5.1 shows the halal control points and control measures in halal warehouse processes for the minimum and preferred levels.

Receiving is one of the most critical halal control points in order to protect the halal integrity of a halal warehouse asset. To my surprise, I am still coming across halal warehouses that have not considered receiving as a halal control point. Missing essential halal control points leads to an unstable halal assurance system for a halal warehouse and will result in potential breakages in your own or your client's halal supply chain.

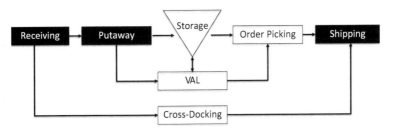

Figure 5.3 Halal warehouse processes.

Table 5.1 Halal control points and control measures in halal warehouse

Halal control points	Halal control measures in halal warehouse	
	Minimum level (non-Muslim country)	Preferred level (Muslim (majority) country)
1. Receiving	Verification of halal status through freight documents and halal certificate; Physical inspection of cargo and packaging for acceptance of goods; Labelling of halal goods as 'HALAL SUPPLY CHAIN' (if not present).	Verification of halal status through freight documents and halal certificate; Non-halal goods are not accepted to enter the halal warehouse facility; Physical inspection of freight and packaging for acceptance of halal goods.
2. Putaway	Label rejected halal goods (based on possible damages, spoilage, breakage, contamination, theft, tempering, etc.) as 'REJECTED'; Move rejected halal goods to quarantine area for further inspection; No mixing of halal with non-halal products on one pallet or load carrier. Move accepted goods to respective storage/VAL/intermediate buffer area.	Label rejected halal goods (based on possible damages, spoilage, breakage, contamination, theft, tempering, etc.) as 'REJECTED'; Move rejected halal goods to quarantine area for further inspection. Move accepted halal goods to storage/VAL/intermediate buffer area.
3. Storage	Halal goods have a dedicated halal storage zone or halal racks; No mixing of halal with non-halal goods vertically; No Mixing of halal with severe najis goods in the same cold room.	not applicable

(Continued)

Table 5.1 (Continued)

Halal control points	Halal control measures in halal warehouse	
	Minimum level (non-Muslim country)	Preferred level (Muslim (majority) country)
4. Value Added Logistics (VAL)	Halal goods have a dedicated VAL area; No combining of halal and non-halal SKUs (Stock Keeping Unit) into a new SKU; No mixing of halal with non-halal products on one pallet or load carrier.	not applicable
5. Cross-docking	Halal goods have a dedicated intermediate buffer area; No mixing of halal with non-halal products on one pallet or load carrier.	not applicable
6. Order picking	No mixing of halal with non-halal products on one pallet or load carrier.	not applicable
7. Shipping	Label 'HALAL SUPPLY CHAIN' cargo sticker on halal goods (if not present); Ensure 'HALAL SUPPLY CHAIN' is coded on freight documents and in IT system for halal cargo; Label 'HALAL SUPPLY CHAIN' container/unit load device/air cargo pallet sticker ONLY on designated halal container/unit load device/air cargo pallet (if not present).	Label 'HALAL SUPPLY CHAIN' cargo sticker on halal goods (if not present); Ensure 'HALAL SUPPLY CHAIN' is coded on freight documents and in IT system; Label 'HALAL SUPPLY CHAIN' container/unit load device/air cargo pallet sticker on designated halal container/unit load device/air cargo pallet (if not present).

Halal transport

Halal transport is the movement of materials, parts, and finished inventory by any modes of transport that are in compliance with shariah. For cargo destined to predominantly Muslim countries, a designated halal transport is needed (preferred level), whereas for cargo destined to non-Muslim countries, mixing of halal and non-halal cargo is to a certain degree possible (minimum level). Although designated halal transport might be easier to manage, this might not be economical in non-Muslim countries. There have been private sector initiatives offering a dedicated halal container (a 20-foot or 40-foot container for halal cargo only), but these companies have been struggling in securing return (halal) cargo. The future will tell if there is a market for dedicated halal containers.

Figure 5.4 shows the halal transport processes: allocation of halal cargo to transport (unit), cleaning of transport (unit), loading in transport (unit), and labelling, and coding. Table 5.2 shows the halal control points and control measures in halal transport processes for the minimum and preferred levels.

Loading in transport (unit) is one of the most critical halal control points in order to protect the halal integrity of halal transport. I am still coming across halal transport solutions that have not considered loading as a halal control point. Missing essential halal control points leads to an unstable halal assurance system for halal transport and potential breakages in your own or your client's halal supply chain.

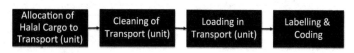

Figure 5.4 Halal transport processes.

Table 5.2 Halal control points and control measures in halal transport

Halal control points	Halal control measures in halal transport	
	Minimum level (non-Muslim country)	Preferred level (Muslim (majority) country)
1. Allocation of halal cargo to transport (unit)	Halal cargo is allocated to a transport (unit); Transport (unit) obtains 'HALAL SUPPLY CHAIN' status ONLY in case of full transport/container/unit load device/air cargo pallet, becoming a designated halal transport	Halal cargo is allocated to a transport (unit); Transport (unit) obtains 'HALAL SUPPLY CHAIN' status, becoming a designated halal transport
2a. Cleaning of transport (unit) - dry unitised	Cleaning according to prevailing hygiene standards;	Cleaning according to prevailing hygiene standards; Ritual cleansing upon request of shipper.
2b. Cleaning of transport (unit) - dry bulk, cool chain (bulk + unitised), and halal livestock	Cleaning according to prevailing hygiene standards;	Cleaning according to prevailing hygiene standards; Ritual cleansing ONLY when applicable to Islamic school of thought of destination country in case of an earlier severe najis or unknown previous shipment; Ritual cleansing upon request of shipper.
3a. Loading in transport (unit) - cargo	No mixing of halal with non-halal bulk cargo; No mixing of halal with non-halal unitised products on one pallet or load carrier; No	No mixing of halal with non-halal bulk cargo; No mixing of halal with non-halal unitised goods in transport (unit).

(Continued)

Table 5.2 (Continued)

Halal control points	Halal control measures in halal transport	
	Minimum level (non-Muslim country)	Preferred level (Muslim (majority) country)
	mixing of halal with severe najis unitised goods in a refrigerated transport (unit).	
3b. Loading in transport (unit) - halal livestock	No mixing of halal with non-halal livestock	No mixing of halal with non-halal livestock
4. Labelling & coding	Label 'HALAL SUPPLY CHAIN' cargo sticker on halal goods (if not present); Ensure 'HALAL SUPPLY CHAIN' is coded on freight documents & IT system for halal cargo. Label 'HALAL SUPPLY CHAIN' container/unit load device/air cargo pallet sticker ONLY on designated halal container/unit load device/air cargo pallet (if not present).	Label 'HALAL SUPPLY CHAIN' cargo sticker on halal goods; Ensure 'HALAL SUPPLY CHAIN' is coded on freight documents and IT system. Label 'HALAL SUPPLY CHAIN' container/unit load device/air cargo pallet sticker on designated halal container/unit load device/air cargo pallet (if not present).

Halal compliant terminal

A halal compliant terminal is a sea, air, or inland terminal where halal goods are segregated from non-halal goods in compliance with shariah. The halal compliant terminal ensures there is physical segregation of halal cargo from non-halal cargo throughout the terminal process.

Figure 5.5 shows the halal compliant terminal processes:

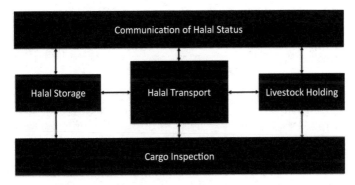

Figure 5.5 Halal compliant terminal process.

communication of halal status, halal transport, halal storage, livestock holding, and cargo inspection. Table 5.3 shows the halal control points and control measures in the halal compliant terminal processes for minimum and preferred levels.

Inspection is an important factor in terminals. It is conducted by an independent party from the terminal operator, such as customs, veterinary services, and other government agencies. Terminals like seaports and airports are national gateways, where nationwide standardisation of halal control points and control measures are of national interest. Therefore, the ministry of transport, or its relevant agencies (like a port authority), should drive the development of halal control points and control measures for its terminals. This cannot be left to the individual terminal operators. Failure to do so will result in inconsistent halal compliant terminal practices within a single country. Inconsistent halal compliant terminal practices lead to variability in halal integrity for halal imports and export chains, weakening a country's halal infrastructure and a country's halal brand.

Table 5.3 Halal control points and control measures in halal compliant terminal

Halal control points	Halal control measures in halal compliant terminal	
	Minimum level (non-Muslim country)	Preferred level (Muslim (majority) country)
1. Communication of halal status	Code 'HALAL SUPPLY CHAIN' cargo status in IT system (under special handling instructions). Track halal certificate of halal cargo. Track and label 'HALAL SUPPLY CHAIN' (container/ unit load device/air cargo pallet sticker) ONLY for designated halal container/unit load device/air cargo pallet (if not present).	Code 'HALAL SUPPLY CHAIN' cargo status in IT system (under special handling instructions). Track halal certificate of halal cargo. Track and label 'HALAL SUPPLY CHAIN' (container/ unit load device/air cargo pallet sticker) for designated halal container/unit load device/air cargo pallet (if not present).
2. Halal transport	Follow halal control points and control measures in halal transport according to **MINIMUM LEVEL**.	Follow halal control points and control measures in halal transport according to **PREFERRED LEVEL**.
3. Halal storage	Halal goods have a designated halal storage zone or halal racks; No mixing of halal with non-halal goods vertically; No Mixing of halal with severe najis goods in the same cold room.	Halal goods have a designated halal storage zone or halal racks; No mixing of halal with non-halal goods vertically; No Mixing of halal with severe najis goods in the same cold room.
4. Livestock holding	No mixing of halal with non-halal livestock in	No mixing of halal with non-halal livestock in

(Continued)

Table 5.3 (Continued)

Halal control points	Halal control measures in halal compliant terminal	
	Minimum level (non-Muslim country)	Preferred level (Muslim (majority) country)
5. **Cargo inspection**	quarantine area and holding yards Inspection of halal cargo at designated halal inspection area. No mixing of halal products with non-halal products on pallet or load carrier at all times and under any conditions.	quarantine area and holding yards Inspection of halal cargo at designated halal inspection area. No mixing of halal products with non-halal products on pallet or load carrier at all times and under any conditions.

Halal retailing

The retailer completes the halal supply chain, where a halal product is handed over to the consumer upon payment. This hand-off is the exact point in the supply chain where the brand owner's halal integrity responsibility ends. This point can be at the retail outlet itself, a collection point for self-pickup, or in case of home delivery at the doorstep of the consumer. After this hand-off, it is the responsibility of the consumer to protect the halal integrity of the halal product from mixing with non-halal, breakage in cool chain, and passing of expiry date.

The goal of halal retailing is to guarantee the halal integrity of a halal category at the point of consumer purchase through effective control of the halal retailing supply chain processes.

Retail today is complex, where retailers are carrying thousands of different stock items, ranging from food (fresh and processed), home care (e.g. fabric cleaners), personal care, paper goods (e.g. toilet paper, diapers), kitchen accessories, magazines, and many more. These products are not only sourced locally but regionally and globally. As margins are relatively low in retailing, there has been a traditional focus on realising cost reductions in storage and transport through consolidation. In practice, consolidation means putting products together based on temperature requirements, not based on the halal status of a product. Mixing of halal and non-halal is an unfortunate consequence.

Although in the food category halal certification has been quite common, in the non-food category this is not the case. It is good to realise that in many supermarkets today only about 30% of the total stock keeping units are actually food, whereas the majority (70%) is non-food. To classify a non-food product as halal or non-halal is not that straight forward as just identifying the pork products and alcoholic beverages. In fact, the product composition needs to be examined in detail, where for animal-based components it is important to know what halal certificate is behind it. What is the Halal Certification Body's reputation, the scope covered in the certification, the halal standard applied, acceptance by the importing country? Furthermore, due to the issuing of fatwas (like the fatwa in January 2019 by JAKIM declaring cigarettes haram), certain retail items can suddenly be declared haram by your local halal authority.

The following halal retailing business models can be differentiated:

- **Halal-exclusive retailer**. The outlet offers halal products only. The halal category is designed to meet the specific needs and halal requirements of the local Muslim community
- **Halal-segregated retailer**. The outlet offers both halal and non-halal products, which are clearly identified and physically segregated in zones, shelves, and/or displays, to address contamination, risk of contamination, and perception issues. The halal category is designed to offer,

as much as possible, a complete halal category to the mainstream Muslim consumer
- **Halal-mixed retailer**. The outlet offers both halal and non-halal products, but are not clearly identified or physically segregated. The retailer does not recognise a halal category as such

All three models can be observed in both Muslim and non-Muslim countries. What are the implications for the retailer for each model?

The halal-exclusive retailer only carries products that are considered halal according to the ruling Islamic school of thought, fatwas, and local customs. A dedicated halal retailer in Malaysia therefore will not carry (products containing) alcoholic beverages, non-halal meat, food products containing animal ingredients that are not halal, cigarettes, and non-food products (such as cosmetics) containing non-halal components. The supply chain to the retailer should be segregated from non-halal (according to its country's halal standards). In the case of home deliveries, halal logistics should be in place up to the consumer doorstep.

A halal-segregated retailer in Muslim-majority countries carries select non-halal products but clearly identifies non-halal products and segregates its physical location throughout the retail supply chain to ensure the halal integrity of the halal category is not compromised. The retailer has 'non-halal zones' for alcoholic beverages and other non-halal food products, like products containing pork meat. A non-halal zone can have its own cashier counter, which is practised by halal-segregated retailers for example in Malaysia. For refrigerated food items, there are paper (preferred) or plastic bags present to prevent contamination of trolleys and cashier counter conveyor belts. On the other hand, it should clearly identify for non-foods if a product is not halal on the shelf itself due to non-compliance of certain components. The supply chain to the retailer should segregate halal from non-halal (according to its country's halal standard). In case of home deliveries, halal logistics services should be offered to ensure that the integrity of halal items is not compromised by mixing halal with non-halal items in the last-mile delivery to the consumer.

For non-Muslim countries, a halal-segregated retailer has a 'halal zone', halal shelves, and/or dedicated halal refrigeration displays. For refrigerated food items, there are paper (preferred) or plastic bags available to prevent contamination. The supply chain to the retailer should segregate halal from non-halal. Staff at halal-segregated retailers should be well-trained to identify the halal and non-halal, avoid mixing at any stage in retail processes, and advise the consumer where to find the halal or non-halal products.

The halal-mixed retailer has not designed a halal category for the Muslim consumer. The implication of this formula is that halal integrity is not assured up to the point of consumer purchaser and identification of halal is left to the assessment by the consumer based on the halal logo and other information stated on the product label. For Muslim countries, this retail formula is not recommended as it provides a major source of corporate reputation risk for both the halal-certified brand owner as well as the retailer (see chapter 10).

Summary – chapter 5: Halal logistics and retailing

- As most of the logistics are outsourced to a logistics service provider, the logistics service provider is a key supply chain partner in extending halal integrity from the source to the point of consumer purchase
- There are halal control points and control measures in the logistics of goods in warehouse, transport, and sea/air/

inland terminals for both Muslim (majority) and non-Muslim countries
- The retailer completes the halal supply chain, where a halal product is handed over to the consumer upon payment. This hand-off is the exact point in the supply chain where the brand owner's halal integrity responsibility ends. There are three halal retailing business models practised: halal-exclusive retailer, halal-segregated retailer, and halal-mixed retailer

Reflection questions

- How are my logistics (storage and transport) organised in both sourcing and distribution?
- Are my logistics service providers halal certified and what halal control points & control measures are put in place by my halal logistics service provider?
- What halal retailing business models are present in my marketing channels?

6

HALAL CLUSTERS

Clustering

The advantages of clustering have been contended by academics since 1890. First by Alfred Marshall, who used the term 'industrial district' which he published in his influential works 'Principles of Economics' in the year 1890 and 'Industry and Trade' in the year 1919. According to Alfred Marshall, the collectivity of specialised firms and the social interdependencies represent the general concept of a cluster. Michael Porter (1990) in 'The Competitive Advantage of Nations' made the definition of cluster broader. Michael Porter defines a cluster as 'A geographically proximate group of interconnected companies and associated institutions in a particular field, linked by commonalities and complementarities'.

In his definition, clusters encompass an array of horizontally and vertically linked industries and other entities important to competition.

Since the publication of the Porter's landmark paper 'Clusters and the New Economics of Competition' in 1998 (Porter 1998), the cluster concept has become a popular framework for academics and practitioners in analysing industrial clusters. According to Porter (2000), clusters increase productivity of industries; increase the capacity of cluster participants for innovation and productivity growth; and stimulate new business formation that supports innovation and expands the cluster. Clusters also create new and better jobs; create new businesses; diversify the local economy; and deliver economic impact (Sheffi 2012).

As highlighted earlier in this book, the halal industry is a fast-growing industry, but has several bottlenecks that hinder the halal industry from going mainstream. There are five major shortcomings in the halal industry. First, there is a shortage of halal ingredients and additives with the appropriate halal certification. Second, there is a lack of high-quality halal production in Muslim countries, even for basic food commodities, which makes Muslim countries highly dependent on imports. This became apparent during the corona crisis of 2020, where Muslim countries were struggling to secure food and medical imports to meet the needs of their citizens. Third, halal industries are fragmented, competing instead of collaborating, and have difficulty upscaling. Fourth, there are few global halal brands from Muslim majority countries present in the halal market, which is currently dominated by multinationals from non-Muslim countries. Fifth, halal is moving away from a product approach and towards a supply chain and value chain approach, which is complex to manage without a halal ecosystem.

If these bottlenecks continue to be unfixed, they will not just limit the full potential of the halal industry, but could even result in a possible collapse of the halal market and international halal trade altogether.

The development of halal clusters should be adopted as the halal industry strategy for Muslim majority countries to better organise and upscale halal production. This will allow Muslim countries to better secure and control the supply of halal products for their citizens and eventually become net exporters.

Halal clusters also have advantages for non-Muslim countries in protecting their export interest with Islamic countries. A halal cluster, part of halal cluster network, could lock-in a supply chain relationship with attractive Muslim markets. Halal ecosystems simplify halal and create synergy advantages for industries serving Muslim markets.

Halal clusters

In line with Michael Porter's cluster definition, I would like to define a halal cluster as 'A geographical concentration of interconnected companies and institutions in a particular halal industry'. Halal clusters can be focused on physical halal production (e.g. halal food, cosmetics, pharmaceuticals, modest fashion), but also on halal services (e.g. halal logistics, Muslim friendly tourism, healthcare, Islamic banking and finance).

Halal clusters facilitate vertical collaboration (within a brand owner supply chain) as well as horizontal collaboration (with organisations that are part of a different supply chain network). Halal synergy advantages can be leveraged by connecting halal clusters together within a country as well as connecting to halal clusters located in other countries. Connecting clusters together facilitates access to halal ingredients, halal markets, halal services, technology, research partners, and many more.

What are the critical components of a halal cluster? A halal cluster is based on five pillars, namely: (1) Muslim consumer; (2) education and research; (3) halal integrity network; (4) halal supply chain; and (5) enablers. The development of these pillars is pivotal in building a sustainable halal cluster. The halal cluster model is shown in figure 6.1.

Muslim consumer

According to the Holy Quran (2:168), the consumption of lawful and good food is an obligation for Muslims. Halal clusters should foremost be value-driven in providing basic Islamic values to the Muslim consumer. Islamic values are shaped by the Islamic school of thought, fatwas, and local customs, which are market specific as discussed in chapter 3. The relationship with local Muslim communities and Muslim consumer associations is also important for solid halal risk and reputation management (chapters 9 and 10).

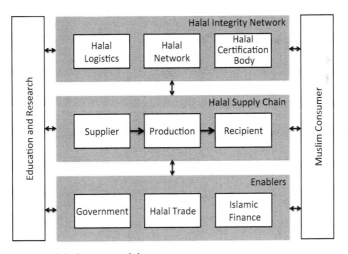

Figure 6.1 Halal cluster model

The halal cluster should be aligned not only to the local halal requirements, the country where the cluster is located, but possible other multiple market requirements based on the various Muslim countries the cluster participants export products.

Education and research

Education and research institutions are the engine of innovation. Cluster research shows that education and research organisations are one of the most critical components of a cluster. In fact, all examples of successful industrial clusters in the world have a top university as an anchor in its cluster. Universities are, therefore, an important catalyst for the innovation and growth of a halal cluster. By bringing the university physically together with the industry, this allows for more focused research based on actual problems and quick implementation of research findings and new discoveries. Other than a university, research is also provided by private research firms. This can be in areas ranging from halal laboratories, research into alternative materials, halal food, medicines, to social sciences.

In order to provide an adequate workforce for a halal cluster, now and in future, both vocational training and academic education are necessary. Vocational training supports practical skill development for employees working for organisations located in the cluster, in areas such as internal halal auditor, halal purchasing, halal logistics, halal supply chain management, halal branding and marketing, Islamic finance, etc.

Universities and colleges could offer specialised academic degrees, depending on the focus of the halal cluster. Close collaboration between universities and colleges with the industry ensures that the curriculum is aligned with industry and cluster needs. On the other hand, students will have ample choice for practical training and graduation projects. Companies can handpick a new generation of workers leaving university after first experiencing the industry during a university project. In other words, a clear win-win situation for both education and industry.

Halal integrity network

The halal integrity network acts as the facilitator to extend halal integrity from source to point of consumer purchase. The halal integrity network consists of halal logistics; halal network; and halal certification body.

Halal logistics provide storage for raw materials and final products. Halal logistics services in a halal cluster supports consolidation of halal cargo to allow for dedicated halal warehouses and designated halal transport, and facilitates vertical and horizontal collaboration across and between supply chain networks (see chapter 5). Depending on the location of the halal cluster, near a national sea or air gateway, there could be a role for a halal regional distribution centre offering consolidation, value added logistics, and distribution activities. There could also be a possible role for a halal supply chain control tower for the management of global flows for halal goods as shared in the previous chapter.

The halal network depends on interpersonal trust and private relationships. A cluster management organisation is thereby pivotal in developing interpersonal trust and private relationships among the cluster participants. The role of the cluster management organisation is to facilitate innovation projects, promote new economic activities, and to reinforce the halal cluster.

Halal clusters are developed bottom-up, originating in a region with a certain kind and amount of existing sustainable advantages. These clusters can include a dedicated halal park or halal zone (part of a larger industrial park). Along with companies based in a halal park (or zone), companies can also be based outside these parks and zones and still be considered to be part of the halal cluster. National and international halal clusters can be connected, forming a global network of halal clusters and halal gateways, transport hubs (seaports and airports) that have halal compliant terminals and halal warehouse facilities, to facilitate efficient local, regional, and global halal trade.

Companies in the halal cluster, could leverage their corporate brand towards a target market based on the halal brand of the country of origin and/or location, for example: 'Halal Saudi Arabia' or 'Halal Medina'; 'Halal Indonesia' or 'Halal Aceh'; 'Halal Malaysia' or 'Halal Johor'; 'Halal UAE' or 'Halal Dubai'; etc. For Muslims, a halal product from a country of origin like the Kingdom of Saudi Arabia, will have a superior perceived halal integrity compared to halal products from Europe or the Americas for instance.

The HCB is an important final component of the halal integrity network as they certify suppliers, production, logistics, and other services according to local as well as international halal standards. To have an HCB located physically in the halal cluster will simplify certification for organisations located in the halal cluster and will be a support for halal issues.

Halal supply chain

A halal supply chain is a network of connected and interdependent organisations mutually and cooperatively working together to manage, control, and improve the flow of materials and information in compliance with the general principles of shariah. When a halal supply chain is physically located inside a halal cluster, the supply chain costs are lower as are lead-times and variability of supply chains.

The presence of internationally competitive ingredient suppliers in a halal cluster creates advantages for downstream industries in several ways. SMEs play a dominant role in developing supply capacity for a country's halal cluster. As securing a supply of ingredients and additives is currently one of the main bottlenecks for many halal industries, a strong emphasis should be made on supplier development of ingredients and additives within the halal cluster.

Second to the access of raw materials, packaging is also an important supplier in halal clusters. Although clusters have a natural pull factor for suppliers, the presence of certain halal ingredients and packaging suppliers will also attract halal manufacturers to be located in a halal cluster. Farms nearby or away from the physical halal cluster can still be critical for the supply of a halal cluster, and therefore still considered part of a halal cluster network. An example of this is Gayo Highlands in Aceh, located on the island of Sumatra (Indonesia), that produces one of the world's best coffee beans. Gayo Highlands is still considered to be part of the 'Modern Halal Valley' halal food cluster network on Java Island (Indonesia), located more than 1,000 miles away.

Production is the core of the halal cluster for supplying halal products to the world. The production in halal clusters should strive for excellence (*ihsan*) in achieving balance with nature (*mizan*). According to Abdul-Matin (2010), a balance with nature particularly addresses waste, energy, and water management. Waste reduction is possible by establishing closed loop production or supply chain systems (Lehr et al 2013), where a by-product is an input for another process. Energy consumption should (to a large extent) be based on renewable energy, namely based on sun and wind energy, instead of non-renewable energy such as oil and coal. Water management should focus the minimisation of water consumption in production, assurance of the quality of water returned to nature, as well as the protection of groundwater (quality).

We urgently need to change the ways in which we run our industrial processes. We are moving away from a traditional paradigm of economies of scale and economies of scope, towards what I would like to call 'economies of chains'. We have to search for new opportunities by linking supply chains to other ecologically fitting supply chains and clusters that increase the business value chain significantly. A good example of this is the coffee chain.

Global coffee consumption today is approximately 155 million bags of coffee (1 bag is 60 kg), of which Asia contributes about 30 million bags and has the highest annual growth. However, harvesting, processing, roasting, and brewing coffee discards an estimated 99.7% of its biomass, while only 0.2% acquires value on the market. Demand for mushrooms has enjoyed double-digit growth for decades. Research shows that farming mushrooms on used coffee grounds is 80% more energy efficient than conventional energy intensive farming methods. In fact, used coffee grounds as the growing medium for mushroom farming is more valuable than a cup of coffee. The rest raw materials from mushroom production, on the other hand, are also excellent raw material for animal feed. By combining the coffee chain with the mushroom and animal feed chains, you can triple or quadruple the economic value of coffee.

Therefore, instead of taking over your competitor, it makes more sense to focus on collaboration, mergers, and acquisitions with organisations that control ecologically fitting supply chains. This is another argument for designated halal parks (or halal zones), where these complex supply chain and processes could be better linked.

As big retail chains are controlling most of consumer retailing today, the involvement of big retailers can be attractive for certain halal clusters. Also, recognising wholesalers and distributors as partners in a halal production cluster contributes to trade facilitation and a better control of halal integrity downstream in the supply chain all the way to the point of consumer purchase.

Enablers

The enablers of a halal cluster are the government, halal trade, and Islamic finance. Governments invest in transport hubs, control the use of land, offer incentives to encourage investments by industries, support education, and provide the regulatory framework for halal clusters and halal parks (or zones). Government policy can positively or negatively influence the competitive advantage of a halal cluster and location for foreign direct investment.

Trade markets provide better control of the supply of halal ingredients and additives. Trading is also needed for international market access, facilitating the import and export of halal products for the halal cluster, and domestic distribution.

Clusters are supported by financial services. Financial infrastructure is part of the supporting cluster infrastructure. Companies in a halal cluster should have access to a variety of Islamic banking, financing, and insurance (*takaful*) products to support the business activities and expansion of the halal cluster. There is also a possible role for *waqf* endowment capital in a halal cluster, for example for financing training and education of local SMEs, as well as poverty alleviation (providing a social safety net) for communities within the radius of the halal cluster. A good example of a halal industry strategy based on the halal cluster philosophy is Malaysia, which is explained in Halal Insight 6.1.

Halal parks and halal zones

Over the years, halal parks and halal zones have been developed in both Muslim-majority and non-Muslim countries. Many of those initiatives have been designed as a dedicated industrial halal park or zone for halal industries, supported by halal certification (body), and government incentives. These halal parks and halal

Halal Insight 6.1 Halal Malaysia

In 1974, the Research Centre of the Islamic Affairs Division of the Prime Minister Office issued its first halal certification letters for products that met halal criteria. In 1994, a halal certification was given in the form of a certificate with a halal logo. On 1 January 1997, in line with the country's steadfast Islamic development and progress, the Department of Islamic Development Malaysia (JAKIM) was established by the Government of Malaysia. Since 2002, all halal certifications activities were conducted by the Malaysian halal authority JAKIM. Today, JAKIM is the sole halal certification body in Malaysia, responsible for the halal certification of food production (including slaughtering), cosmetics and personal care, pharmaceuticals, medical devices, leather products, logistics, and retail. The certification is based on halal standards developed by Department of Standards Malaysia, which can be audited by the various State Islamic Religious Affairs Councils or JAKIM themselves, and be certified by JAKIM only.

JAKIM is one of the most established HCBs in the world, and its reputation is respected globally. JAKIM keeps a list of HCBs approved by them, which is used globally by governments and other HCBs to ensure the recognised credibility of HCBs on their list. Under the Third Industrial Master Plan (IMP3: 2006–2020), Malaysia is positioned to become the global halal hub for the production and trade in halal goods and services, where Malaysia can be one of the leading suppliers of halal products and services. From the Ninth Malaysian Plan (RMK9), the Halal Industry Development Corporation (HDC) was formed on 18 September 2006 to coordinate overall development of the halal industry in Malaysia with the vision to make Malaysia the global halal hub. HDC is a completely government-owned organisation. The role of HDC is to (1) lead the development of halal standards, audit and certification procedures in order to protect the integrity of Halal; (2) direct and coordinate the development of Malaysia's halal industry amongst all stake holders - both public and private; (3) manage capacity building for halal producers and related service providers; (4) support investment into Malaysia's halal industry; (5) facilitate the growth and participation of Malaysian companies in the global Halal market; (6) develop, promote, and market the Malaysian halal brand; and (7) promote the concept of halal and related goods and services.

Malaysia has four industry focus areas: specialty processed food, cosmetics and personal care, ingredients, and animal husbandry. HDC established a dedicated set of attractive incentives for halal park operators, halal industry players, and halal logistics service providers. The halal parks were an important part of HDC industry strategy in clustering halal industries in Malaysia, providing clustering advantages and financial incentives for industries located in these parks. Today, Malaysia has more than 20 halal parks, of which some have a more international focus, whereas others focus on a domestic role. HDC introduced the HALMAS status, an accreditation given to halal park operators who have successfully complied with the requirements and guidelines stipulated under the HDC designated Halal Park Development. Next to local companies, these halal parks are also home to multinational companies such as Coco-Cola. In 2020, the dairy multinational company FrieslandCampina announced to move its Malaysian dairy plant to the halal park Techpark@Enstek, which is entirely owned by Lembaga Tabung Haji, Malaysia's Pilgrims' Fund Board.

Malaysia is an important base for MNC food companies to produce halal products for the world under the 'halal Malaysia' brand, leveraging on the rich agriculture resources in and around Malaysia. Furthermore, it has a strong logistics service sector that has been proactive in developing halal

> logistics capabilities. This also includes some halal compliant terminal initiatives at its main sea ports and airports in Malaysia. The Malaysian government, supported by leading Islamic scholars and financial institutions, are taking steps to turn Kuala Lumpur, Malaysia's capital, into a global hub for Islamic finance.
>
> Malaysia's long history in Islamic finance started with an Islamic fund management company in 1962 under 'Pilgrim's Management Fund' or 'Lembaga Tabung Haji', followed in 1983 by the first Malaysian Islamic bank 'Bank Islam'. Malaysia has several leading universities and research institutes that conduct research in halal food science; halal logistics and supply chain management; Islamic finance; and Islamic marketing.
>
> Malaysia is one of the few countries today that are in the third phase of the halal evolution 'halal supply chain', as it has a complex set of local standards (covering production as well as logistics and retailing). Malaysia has a strong cluster foundation due to (1) its leading position in the Islamic World and OIC on halal matters; (2) supply of raw materials (mainly palm oil), supporting infrastructure and technology; (3) global recognition of its halal standards and halal authority JAKIM; and (4) strong government commitment. Malaysia is home to the World Halal Forum, World Halal Conference, and halal exhibition MIHAS, which are important established platforms for the global halal society.

zones were not designed as a halal eco-system, providing insufficient halal synergy advantages for industries to be located in or relocate to these halal parks or halal zones. As a result, many halal parks (and halal zones) today are not successful. A few exceptions are those halal parks (and halal zones) located next to an international logistics gateway (seaport or airport), but their success might be related more to their location, providing logistical advantages, rather than their actual halal business or operating model.

I still believe that in order to solve the bottlenecks in the halal supply chain, and to support the growth of the halal industry, there is a key role for halal parks and halal zones. These halal parks and halal zones will need to be designed differently, to be reinvented as halal clusters instead. Halal parks and halal zones should provide a superior halal ecosystem for industries to create a pull factor for halal industries to move to these halal parks (or zones).

A halal park is a spatial clustering of halal production chains in an industrial park or economic zone, wherein a significant part of the halal cluster is positioned inside the halal park (or zone). Therefore, the halal ecosystem of a halal park extends beyond the physical boundaries of the halal park itself, orchestrated by a halal cluster organisation. The halal cluster organisation ensures the development of the cluster itself and connecting to other clusters within and outside the country. The goal of a halal park (or zone) is to generate synergy advantages for industries located in these halal parks (or zones).

What is the value for industries to locate in a halal park or halal zone?

- A complete halal eco-system for industries to simplify halal operations
- Access to raw materials, supply and supporting industry through farmer and SME programmes under a premium halal brand
- Market access to attractive local and export markets
- Access to a well-educated labour force
- Excellent location and connectivity via road, sea, air, etc.

Modern Halal Valley in Indonesia, near the capital Jakarta, is an example of a halal park based on halal cluster principles. It is designed as a halal food+ cluster, with a Halal Valley Society as cluster management organisation. Figure 6.2 shows the layout design of Modern Halal Valley.

In the year 2019, Modern Halal Valley founded the Halal Cluster Network, connecting Modern Halal Valley to other halal clusters in the world. The Halal Cluster Network links local, regional, and international halal clusters together in a halal cluster network.

The Halal Cluster Network adds value to its partners through:

- **Halal Synergy Advantages** through collaboration
- **Effective Halal Assurance** based on the international halal logistics standard and consistent communication of the halal status on freight documents, labels, and electronic communication

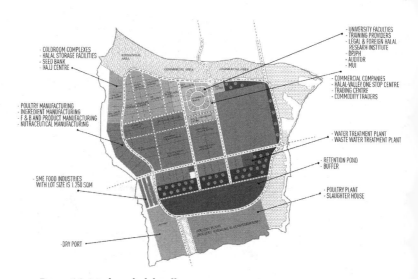

Figure 6.2 Modern halal valley
Source: PT. Modern Industrial Estat

- **Creating a green lane** for halal imports, exports and domestic distribution in partner countries
- **Joint promotion** of halal clusters and international halal trade between halal clusters
- **Access to a sourcing network** for halal raw materials, ingredients, and additives
- **Access to export markets** of intermediate and final products
- **Knowledge sharing, joint industry projects,** and **research and development**

In summary, halal parks and halal zones should be based on a halal cluster design to enable them to create a superior halal eco-system for halal industries to ensure the growth of the halal cluster.

Summary – chapter 6: Halal cluster

- A halal cluster is a geographical concentration of interconnected companies and institutions in a particular halal industry. Halal clusters can be focused on physical halal production (e.g. halal food, cosmetics, pharmaceuticals, modest fashion) and halal services (e.g. halal logistics, Muslim friendly tourism, healthcare, Islamic banking and finance)
- A halal cluster model is based on five pillars, namely: (1) Muslim consumer; (2) education and research; (3) halal integrity network; (4) halal supply chain; and (5) enablers
- The development of halal clusters should be adopted by governments as halal industry strategy for predominantly Muslim countries to better organise and elevate halal production. Halal clusters also have advantages for non-Muslim countries in protecting their export interest with Islamic countries. Halal ecosystems simplify halal and create synergy advantages for industries in serving Muslim markets

- There is an important role for halal parks and halal zones in both Muslim-majority and non-Muslim countries to address existing bottlenecks in halal supply chains and support the fast growth of the halal industry

Reflection questions

- In which (halal) industries does my country have an international competitive advantage?
- What are my sources of competitive advantage for the halal industry? Is there an existing geographical concentration present of this industry?
- Does a halal park or halal zone provide synergy advantages for my organisation and supply chain (partners)?

References

Abdul-Matin, I., 2010. GreenDeen: What Islam Teaches About Protecting the Planet. Berrett-Koehler Publishers, San Francisco.

Lehr, C. B., Thun, J. H., Milling, P. M., 2013. From waste to value–A system dynamics model for strategic decision-making in closed-loop supply chains. International Journal of Production Research 51 (13), 4105–4116. https://doi.org/10.1080/00207543.2013.774488.

Porter, M.E., 1990. The competitive advantage of nations. The Free Press, New York.

Porter, M. E., 1998. Clusters and the new economics of competition. Harvard Business Review 76 (6), 77–90.

Porter, M. E., 2000. Location, competition, and economic development: Local clusters in a global economy. Economic Development Quarterly 14 (1), 15–34. https://doi.org/10.1177/089124240001400105.

Sheffi, Y., 2012. Logistics Clusters: Delivering Value and Driving Growth. Massachusetts Institute of Technology, MIT Press, London.

PART III

HALAL BRANDING AND MARKETING

7

HALAL BRANDING

Halal trust

Evidently, trust in halal is an important factor for the Muslim consumer in purchasing their daily needs. Several academic studies have been undertaken, based on consumer surveys among Muslims consumers, to understand factors that determine purchase intention of halal products. In these studies, the world 'trust' is often mentioned as critical. Trust is considered an independent variable or moderating variable influencing purchase intention. Trust has been frequently defined as the consumer trust in the halal logo of a halal certification body (HCB).

A higher level of halal trust in these studies has been associated with HCBs from Muslim-majority countries.

Several multinational consumer product manufacturers, coffee chains, and fast-food chains measure the halal confidence of their products among Muslim consumers through periodic surveys. What is halal trust exactly and what are the appropriate criteria to measure halal trust?

I would like to define halal trust as 'The belief of the Muslim consumer in the halal integrity of the product or service in accordance with his or her faith'.

The building blocks of halal trust are proposed in figure 7.1 through the Halal Trust Iceberg. The visible component of halal trust is the halal logo, but also other building blocks determine the Muslim consumer trust in a brand, namely excellence, transparency, halal authenticity, and intention/honesty. How can we best measure the halal trust of the Muslim consumer in a brand? Halal Insight 7.1 proposes a possible measurement instrument.

Branding halal

Traditionally, the halal status was assumed for all non-pork food products and non-alcoholic beverages available in predominantly Muslim countries. Halal certification bodies changed this precept, however, by issuing halal certificates for food and non-food products based on an assessment of ingredients/materials used and production/operations processes. This allowed brand owners to place a halal logo on their products, outlets, or services.

Today in the supermarket you can observe a great diversity of halal logos used due to the presence of imported items sold by retailers. It is not easy for Muslim consumers to understand the difference between the various halal logos, to determine the amount of trust they should place in a specific halal logo,

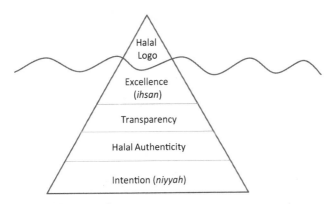

Figure 7.1 Halal trust iceberg

and, of course, the halal integrity of a product based on their own beliefs, such as how an animal is slaughtered. Some predominantly Muslim countries, like Indonesia, have taken regulatory action prohibiting consumer products to carry any halal logo other than their country's own. Most Muslim countries, however, have not followed this example. As a result, in supermarkets today you not only find a greater diversity of halal logos on the supermarket shelves, but even within a single corporate brand, you see different halal logos being used because of the lack of harmonisation. Labelling a product, outlet, or service as halal does not just mean permissible; it also says that the product and its processes are religiously pure (Wilson 2018).

The goal of branding a product halal is to communicate to the consumer that the product has been verified halal by an independent Halal Certification Body (HCB). There are three possible ways to communicate this, through halal co-branding, halal ingredient branding, and halal-coding.

Seeking opportunities in the rapidly growing halal market, companies are increasingly using halal co-branding when

Halal Insight 7.1 Halal trust measurement

Measuring the halal trust of a brand through a consumer survey assesses the consumer perception of the halal logo, excellence, transparency, halal authenticity, and intention. The following Likert scale measurement tool is proposed:

Halal logo

The credibility of a halal certificate: the level of trust in the halal certification body and its standard, could be measured by:

- I trust [company name]'s halal certificate
- I admire and respect [name HCB] halal certificate
- I prefer [name HCB] to the halal certification of other certifiers

Excellence (ihsan)

Halal and quality excellence could be measured by:

- I believe that [company name] performs at the highest level of [food/product safety]
- The company is producing [product category] that are religiously pure
- This company has an excellent halal reputation

Transparency

Evidence supports from previous halal crises that transparency is crucial. Transparency could be measured by:

- I believe what this company says
- [company name] makes truthful halal claims
- This is one of the best halal-certified companies

Halal authenticity

What is the halal DNA of the company? Halal authenticity can be measured by:

- [company name] has a halal policy
- The company is aligned with the values, norms, and ideals of the Muslim faith
- I believe that this company is exceeding existing halal standards

Intention (niyyah)

Intention is the foundation of halal trust. Intention and honesty of a company can be measured by:

- I admire and respect this company
- [company name] is honest
- [company name] is respectful of Islamic law.

---

marketing their products to Muslims. Halal co-branding is practised when 'halal', 'Islamic' or 'shariah' (Islamic law) are jointly used with a corporate brand on a product, outlet or service. Shariah compliance, symbolised by the halal logo, is foregrounded during the branding exercise with the goal of harvesting brand synergy advantages. Wilson (2018) defines this category as a 'halal brand', where a branded product or outlet is clearly positioned, signalled, and communicated to be aligned with the values, norms, and ideals of the Muslim faith. Examples of companies that do this in Malaysia are KFC and McDonalds; in Indonesia, the cosmetics company Wardah does the same.

Halal ingredient branding, on the other hand, considers the halal logo part of the product label, equal to product quality certificates. Halal ingredient branding emphasizes the halal compliance of the product for the Muslim consumer. The halal logo is present, but on the product label instead of the front of the product packaging; or in case of an outlet, mentioned somewhere on the menu and/or a halal certificate displayed at the outlet; or in case of a service, listed together with other quality certificates. A halal logo and status are not promoted explicitly in commercials and advertising.

A third option, not yet being practised, is halal-coding. This approach is currently used for Kosher labelling. Kosher uses the symbol 'K' with optional additional words—'Pareve' (neutral), 'D' or 'Dairy' (products containing dairy), 'DE' (dairy equipment), or 'P' (Passover dietary laws) — to signal when something complies with Jewish dietary laws. Within the halal context, instead of showing a halal logo, a halal code could be used on product labels or food menus — the letter 'H', for example, followed by additional symbols indicating a halal authority (e.g. 'H Jakim'), a slaughtering process (e.g. 'H 01' for hand slaughtered, no stunning), or 'H Vegan' for vegan halal products.

Next to traditional halal-certified industries like food, cosmetics, and pharmaceuticals, other consumer products and industrial brand owners want to carry a halal logo, including fashion, cat food, refrigerators, paint, chemicals, and many more. It is logical that halal compliance is a market qualifier for doing business in Muslim markets, being essential for protecting Muslim consumers as well as the corporate halal reputation of brand owners.

There are however important philosophical questions. Are there possible risks in over-branding halal? Is there not a danger that the actual needs of the consumer are overlooked, creating resentment towards a brand, or potentially scaring consumers away? Instead of creating a stronger corporate halal authenticity, are companies not destroying halal values instead?

Over-branding in Muslim (majority) countries occurs when:

- Halal co-branding is used for products that are not good (for example, products that are nutritionally deficient, harmful to the body, use child labour, or pollute our waterways). Once discovered or exposed, brand owners could see their products rejected by Muslims and see their sales drop
- Halal co-branding is used for products and services for which halal certification is not essential to protect the Muslim way of life. This might create doubt about the intention of the brand owners and scare Muslim consumers away. The same could be true when the halal logo is branded extensively on a category of products or services new to halal certification
- Halal co-branding is used when halal compliance is not considered beyond the first tier of the supply chain – that is, only between the first-tier supplier and the first-tier customer; instead of the entire end-to-end halal supply chain. This could expose the halal integrity of a product. This last category of over-branding halal will particularly affect brands that originate from non-Muslim countries (also known as inbound Islamic brands)

When halal is over-branded in non-Muslim countries, there could also be negative reactions from non-Muslims and even halal boycotts, such as what happened in Europe over the past years. Over-branding in non-Muslim countries could damage both the corporate reputation of halal-certified brand owners and the general perception of halal among non-Muslims. This could reduce the availability of halal products in non-Muslim countries, resulting in hardship for Muslims trying to procure their daily needs. Research shows that negative reactions are predominantly happening in non-Muslim countries where there is no halal regulation.

Halal ingredient branding is in principle the norm for branding halal on products. However, halal-coding is more effective than halal ingredient branding in non-Muslim countries without a halal law (through a Halal Act or Labelling Law) and government accredited halal certification bodies. Halal co-branding is more effective than halal ingredient branding in Muslim (majority) countries for food, nutrition, beverages, and cosmetics that go into the mouth; products that are good and where brand owners take a halal supply chain approach. Figure 7.2 summarises how best to brand halal in predominantly Muslim and non-Muslim countries. It is necessary to realise that branding halal is purely a branding and marketing decision, whereas the decision of halal certification is a pure risk management decision.

Halal brand equity assets

Building a strong brand in Muslim markets requires careful planning and long-term investment. Brand building in Muslim

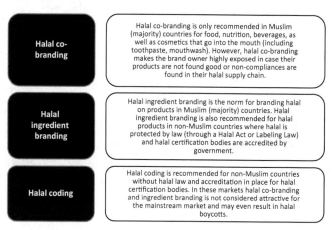

Figure 7.2 Branding halal

markets is the result of an ongoing, steady stream of consistent small efforts, not a series of one-off, gigantic pushes. Branding is a marathon that builds your track record that validates who you are and where you have come from (Leland 2016). In order to be a leader in Muslim markets, you need to rise to such a level of excellence that the Muslim consumer will seek out your brand as a recognised authority.

Halal brand equity are the added Islamic values endowed to products and services. The Islamic value may be reflected in how consumers think, feel, and act with respect to your brand. Halal brand equity is an important intangible asset to the firm that has a financial but also psychological value.

The challenge for marketers is building a brand that ensures that the Muslim consumer has the right type of experience with their products or services. A brand is, in essence, a promise to deliver a predictable product or service performance. For companies to build iconic brands in Muslim markets, they must connect with local cultural knowledge, understand Islamic principles, and hire the best experts.

There are three types of halal brand equity asset classifications that can be differentiated:

- **Halal commodity** – This refers to natural commodities, such as palm oil, dates, rice, fruit, tea, coffee, cocoa, and minerals. Yet, no brands from OIC countries with a global standing exist in this category. Among the regional brands with potential in this category are, for example, Astra from Indonesia, and IOI and Sime Darby from Malaysia; but these palm oil companies lack focus and synergy, as they are too diversified in their business portfolio
- **Potential halal asset** – This refers to building a global brand from scratch. For this category, there are few brands from OIC countries with a global standing. In oil and gas, we have

Aramco from Saudi Arabia and Petronas from Malaysia. In airlines, there are big brands like Emirates (UAE), Saudia (Saudi Arabia), Turkish Airlines (Turkey), Qatar Airways (Qatar), and Garuda Indonesia (Indonesia). What global brands from OIC countries are there in food, cosmetics, pharmaceuticals, fashion, or in banking and finance?

- **Acquired halal asset** – This refers to a taking over a global brand and 'halalise' the brand. For example, the UAE government could decide to buy the food multinational Nestlé in Switzerland and turn Nestlé into a halal brand or a purely halal food business using the UAE halal standard worldwide; or buy the American coffee chain Starbucks and transform it into a halal brand, or a purely halal food business, all over the world based on the UAE halal standard

Building and managing halal brand equity assets requires a long-term approach to branding decisions. As halal brand equity is a valuable asset for the company, this needs to be carefully managed so that its value does not depreciate. Reinforcing halal brand equity requires innovation and relevance for the Muslim consumer. The brand must be moving in the right direction. This requires consistency in marketing support the brand receives to maintain strategic thrust and direction of the brand.

One of the most important decisions in branding is the brand name for a product or service. It is worthwhile to explore the possible use of a local (contextual) Islamic or an Arabic name. For example, if your company logo is an apple, you could call your company 'Apple' or the Arabic name for apple 'Tafaha'. It is extremely important to explore the broader meaning of the Arabic word, historical use, importance in Islam, and possible positive or negative associations. You should also be mindful of the pronunciation and meaning of your foreign brand name or company name in the local language and in Arabic. Negative associations should be avoided at all costs.

Halal brand positioning

The positioning of a brand is about crafting a corporate image to occupy a distinctive place in the mind of the target market. How can brands differentiate themselves in the halal markets? There are two dimensions which are important in brand differentiation. First, based on the origin of the brand (Alserhan 2010): 'Does the brand originate from an Islamic country or non-Islamic country?' Second, based on the halal branding (Wilson 2018): 'Does the brand owner position the brand as a halal brand or halal product (or service)?' Combining both perspectives results in a halal brand positioning matrix with four distinctive quadrants as shown in figure 7.3.

A halal brand is a brand that is clearly positioned, signalled, and communicated to be aligned with the values, norms, and

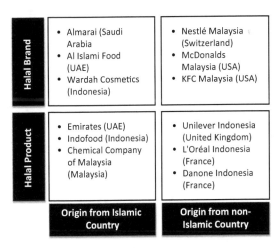

Figure 7.3 Halal brand positioning matrix

ideals of the Muslim faith (Wilson 2018). A halal brand targets the Muslim consumer. A halal product (or service) on the other hand, ensures shariah compliance of the product (or service), its supply chain, and possibly even its value chain. A halal product does not necessarily target the Muslim consumer. There are clear examples of companies in each quadrant.

Although it is not necessary for a halal brand to incorporate an Arabic script into its brand, there could be halal branding advantages in Muslim markets using Arabic or local Muslim names. Therefore, if you are launching a new product (or existing product but slightly different) in the Muslim market, it is good to research if there is an Arabic word you could use instead. It is interesting to note that Emirates has incorporated the Arabic script, although it is not positioned as a halal brand.

What are the attributes or benefits consumers strongly associate with the brand that they could not find to the same extent with a competitive brand? How does it contribute to the Islamic lifestyle? How central are Islamic values to the identity of a brand? Creating strong Islamic associations as a point of difference is essential in terms of competitive brand positioning for halal brands in particular. In terms of competitive advantage, leverageable advantages can be obtained by personnel differentiation (Muslim staff in front-line positions, a strategy which is used by companies in Malaysia); channel differentiation (by controlling an end-to-end channel by a brand; or using halal only sales and distribution channels); or image differentiation (traditional Muslim, modern Muslim, Muslim, and non-Muslim). In terms of point of parity, it is important for brands operating in a halal market to communicate that the product is halal (certified), representing essential conditions for brand choice in Muslim markets.

Summary – chapter 7: Halal branding

- Halal trust can be defined as the belief of the Muslim consumer in the halal integrity of the product or service in accordance with his or her faith. The building blocks of halal trust are the halal logo, excellence, transparency, halal authenticity, and intention
- The goal of branding a product halal is to communicate to the consumer that the product has been verified halal by an independent halal certification body (HCB). There are three possible ways to communicate this: halal co-branding, halal ingredient branding, or halal-coding. Branding halal is purely a branding and marketing decision, whereas having halal certification is a risk management decision
- Halal brand equity is the added Islamic values endowed to products and services. There are three halal brand equity asset classifications: halal commodity, potential halal asset, and acquired halal asset
- The positioning of a brand is about crafting a corporate image to occupy a distinctive place in the mind of the target market. A halal brand positioning matrix has been introduced, based on two dimensions: (1) 'Does the brand originate from an Islamic country or non-Islamic country?'; (2) 'Does the brand owner position the brand as a halal brand or halal product (or service)?'

Reflection questions

- What is the halal trust of my brand among Muslim consumers?
- What is the best halal branding strategy for my products in Muslim (majority) and non-Muslim countries?
- How can I best build and manage my brand equity assets in Muslim markets?

References

Alserhan, B. A., 2010. On Islamic branding: brands as good deeds. *Journal of Islamic Marketing* 1 (2), 101–106. https://doi.org/10.1108/17590831011055842.

Leland, K. T., *The Brand Mapping Strategy: Design, Build, and Accelerate your Brand*, Entrepreneur Press, New York.

Wilson, J. A. J., 2018. *Halal Branding*, Claritas Books, Swansea.

8

HALAL MARKETING

Halal marketing strategy

The essence of halal marketing covers those activities undertaken by an organisation in identifying and meeting the needs of the Muslim consumer. For halal marketing, high-touch engagements with the Muslim consumer are essential for developing and maintaining halal trust. In the book Marketing 4.0 written by Philip Kotler, Hermawan Kartajaya, and Iwan Setiawan, the authors argue that connectivity is the most important game-changer in the history of marketing (Kotler et al. 2017). Central in connectivity is the collaboration with competitors and co-creation with customers. In embracing connectivity, the authors differentiate mobile connectivity (through mobile devices); experiential connectivity (internet is used to deliver a superior customer experience in touchpoints between customer and brands); and the ultimate level of social connectivity (strength of connection in communities of customers). Direct social connectivity with Muslim societies are recommended strategies in halal marketing. Social connectivity also creates a perfect environment for customer advocacy of brands and strengthens halal reputation (chapter 10). Market segmentation, value chain and value network, and marketing channels are core marketing concepts that are particularly important for halal marketing.

Market segmentation

While religious demography is a useful starting point for segmentation, it is severely limited in its scope. As also highlighted by other authors, 'The Muslim' does not exist. Muslims are diverse, ranging from tribal cultures in the Middle East, Muslims that are part of a cultural melting pot in Asia, to hipsters in western urban metropolis, and many more. Maybe more useful segmentation criteria are the benefits sought/problems solved, occasion/context of the purchase, usage of the product or service, and loyalty (Leboff 2020).

Similar to other markets, market research and demand forecasting are important for identifying the actual consumer needs in the halal market. The challenge is that many Islamic countries are not high-income countries, therefore secondary market data is often limited. Primary market data gathering is often needed.

Halal value chain and networks

As mentioned by Warren Buffet, 'Price is what you pay. Value is what you get'. Good marketing generates incremental value, increases the brand's value perception, and generates positive returns (Lamelas 2016). In other words, what value does your product or service add to the consumer? How does the product or service add value to the Muslim lifestyle and obligations?

If we talk about a halal value chain, in essence, it is a discussion about the actual halal DNA of a company. How are Islamic principles and values integrated by the company? We do not mean just halal compliance, but all components of the business DNA. Is there a strategic fit between corporate resources and capabilities and the needs of the Muslim markets? The value chain concept, as developed by Michael Porter (1985), disaggregated a firm into its strategically relevant activities as a potential source of differentiation. The value chain identifies primary value activities: inbound logistics, operations, outbound logistics, marketing and sales, and service. Second, the value chain recognises supporting activities: procurement, technology development, human resource development, and firm infrastructure. Within each primary and support activity, there are four activity types that play a different role in competitive advantage:

- **Direct process activities:** activities directly involved in creating value for the Muslim consumer
- **Indirect process activities:** activities that make it possible to perform direct activities
- **Quality assurance activities:** quality control activities that ensure the quality (goodness) of direct and indirect activities
- **Halal assurance activities:** halal control measures that ensure the halal integrity of direct and indirect activities

In creating a correct-consistent-complete-clear (C4) corporate halal value chain, it requires a review of the direct process activities and indirect process activities, and defining the quality assurance and halal assurance activities for each primary and supporting activity. When considering linking a company's halal value chain with its supply chain partners and alliances that the firm creates to source, make, and deliver its halal product and services, we talk about an entire halal value network. Strong supply chain linkages and associations result in marketing power.

You can argue that the Muslim consumer is part of this network, the consumer is the starting point of a halal value network rather than the end. A brand owner is orchestrating this halal value network to deliver superior value to its various Muslim markets.

Halal marketing channels

Are dedicated halal marketing channels necessary? There is an increasing number of dedicated B2B halal trading portals as well as online halal consumer market places. However, with regard to the logistics, many dedicated halal market places do not provide end-to-end halal supply chain management solutions. On the other hand, there are also conventional B2B trading platforms that are offering halal logistics as an option. For C4 halal trading, a trading portal should facilitate end-to-end halal supply chains.

For the top performance of halal marketing channels to determine the goals per halal marketing channel, they must determine the rules of a marketing channel programme (including halal market requirements), decide on a suitable reward system (not based on interest, ambiguity, and speculation), check that costs and benefits distribution is fair, implement the marketing channel programme, and evaluate the channel performance (Kester 2000).

The development of a measurement and monitoring system provides intelligence on the halal market and the marketing channel performance. Measuring the channel performance is

HALAL MARKETING 125

Table 8.1 Marketing channel performance metrics (example)

		Value	Points	Value	Points	Score	Weight	Result (score x weight)
A	**Marketing channel (analysis per market channel)**							
1	Annual revenue	>= 10,000,000.-	100	< 10,00,000.-	0		25	
2	Annual revenue growth	>= 10%	100	< 10%	0		25	
3	Profitability	>= 15%	100	< 15%	0		25	
4	Market share	>= 10%	100	< 10%	0		25	
							100	
B	**Market requirements (parameters per market channel)**	Value	Tick	Value	Tick			
1	Islamic country	YES		NO				
2	Halal certification mandatory or competitive advantage	YES		NO				
3	Halal maturity of marketing channel	Muslim company, Halal Product		Halal Supply Chain, Halal Value Chain				
C	**Channel partner (analysis per channel partner per market channel)**	Value	Points	Value	Points	Score	Weight	Result (score x weight)
1	Classification of channel partner	Halal certified or SOPs	100	No halal SOPs	0		25	

(Continued)

Table 8.1 (Continued)

						Points	Score	Weight	Result (score x weight)
2	Classification of channel partner logistics service provider	Halal certified or SOPs		100	No halal SOPs	0		25	
3	Last physical halal audit results	NO ISSUES		100	ISSUES	0		25	
4	Halal incidents or halal related complaints over the past 12 months	NONE		100	YES	0		25	
								100	
D	**Product category (analysis per product per market channel)**	**Value**	**Points**		**Value**	**Points**	**Score**	**Weight**	**Result (score x weight)**
1	Revenue	>= 100,000.-		100	< 100,000.-	0		15	
2	Gross margin	>= 30%		100	< 30%	0		15	
3	Direct product profitability	>= 15%		100	< 15%	0		10	
4	Number of customers per year	>= 100		100	< 100	0		10	
5	Number of orders per month	>= 50		100	< 50	0		5	
6	Traffic (fast, medium, or slow mover)	A or B article		100	C or D article	0		5	

(Continued)

Table 8.1 (Continued)

7	Replacement product offered in the category or product range	Not available	100	Available	5
8	Strategic importance of product in category or product range	Top 20	100	Bottom 80	5
9	Halal certified	YES	100	NO	20
10	Benefit to Muslim lifestyle and obligations	HIGH	100	LOW	10
					100

based on objective performance indicators. A possible marketing channel performance metrics are shown in table 8.1.

The metrics provide an assessment of the marketing channel, market requirements, channel partners, and product categories. The marketing channel includes an analysis per market of annual revenue, annual revenue growth, profitability, and market share. The market requirements have three parameters: (1) Islamic country; (2) halal certification mandatory or competitive advantage; and (3) halal maturity of market channel. The values here determine the weights under sections C and D.

Channel partner performance evaluation assesses the halal classification (halal-certified, halal SOPs, no halal SOPs) of both channel partners as well as the channel partner's logistics service provider. Performance monitoring is complemented by physical halal audits. The frequency of audit is determined by the risk profile as will be discussed in the next chapter (chapter 9), but mainly answers the question, 'Were there any halal incidents or halal related complaints over the past 12 months?'.

Product category performance evaluates each product (or stock-keeping unit) for its performance based on ten criteria. For online market channels, this evaluation needs to be done frequently, e.g. monthly. This is essential as you need to react fast in an online market, which is unpredictable and volatile. For offline market channels, this could be done less frequently, e.g. quarterly.

Poor channel performance triggers possible modifications in (1) category offered in marketing channel; (2) channel partners; and (3) marketing channel design. Results of 50 and above require no action. Results of 26–49 require investigations to analyse the reasons behind low scores and assess potential for increasing scores. Sales could, for example, provide their expert opinion if it is possible to turn poor sales performance around for certain products, and come up with an action plan to improve these scores. Scores of 25 or below, suggest an exit of products, channel partners, or even marketing channels.

Values and weights in this table require careful design and calibration, which is determined by testing with historical data and consensus from the management team: CEO, marketing (category management), sales, procurement, production, and logistics. The values and weights need to be finetuned at least annually and in case of major market shifts, or extreme low or high overall results.

Halal marketing channels are characterised by simple halal marketing channel structures, high level of coordination (vertical and horizontal), and low level of channel conflict (due to extensive contracts and training).

Halal services marketing

Services marketing is different from product marketing. Services are processes consisting of (a series of) purely activities. Services cannot be stored, as they are produced and consumed simultaneously. To some extent, the consumer participates as a co-producer in the service production (value creation) process. The quality of a service is as good as it has been experienced or perceived during the last service performance. Service quality and halal excellence are therefore even more important for the effective marketing of services. Halal services have seen a fast growth over the past years, covering a wide range of services, such as food services, logistics, hospitality, healthcare, tourism, Islamic banking and finance, media, consultancy, training, and research. Halal Insight 8.1 provides insight into an example of halal services: the shariah-compliant and Muslim-friendly hotel.

Whereas product marketing, is very much based on transactional marketing, services marketing is based more on relationship marketing. Relationship marketing requires the integration of distinct communication and interaction processes into one systematically implemented strategy. Only this ensures an ongoing relationship between the company and its customer, and dialogue is maintained (Gronroos 2007).

In service delivery, key building blocks in halal services marketing are:

- **Customer contact:** In the offering of a halal service, the front-line staff is involved in the service delivery. The Muslim consumer can see the other person, where attired and personal appearance, behaviour, and speech can be observed. A front-line staff who is scarcely dressed with unclean clothes, and behaves in a rude and vulgar manner, will damage your halal service marketing. In Malaysia, a Muslim country, restaurants prefer to put Muslims in front-line positions as the cashier and waiter, whereas in the kitchen (out of sight) this is not necessarily the case. The restaurants hope to create hereby a halal image through its front-line staff. This strategy is also used by the multinationals McDonald's and Starbucks in Malaysia
- **Systems and operational routines:** Operational processes and routines directly influence the quality and halal perception of the customer. Operational processes and routines should meet the highest quality and halal standards as these are transparent and inspected by the customer personally in every encounter. Mistakes in halal control points and control measures are in the open. A robust design of the halal assurance system is thereby pivotal for services organisations
- **Halal assets:** Halal assets consist of people, equipment and tools, and the facility (outlet). People need to be well-trained on halal as the interaction between the customer and the organisation is face-to-face, personal, and intensive. The customer can be testing and interrogating a front-line worker

Halal Insight 8.1 Shariah-compliant and Muslim-friendly hotel

Muslim travelers are seeking essential faith-based needs when they travel. This includes halal food, prayer, hygienic bathroom facilities, services, and facilities during Ramadan, facilities with no forbidden activities, and recreational facilities with privacy. Two main classifications are available for hospitality services: shariah-compliant hotel and Muslim friendly hotel.

Shariah-compliant hotel

A shariah-compliant hotel fulfills the needs of the Muslim traveler according to shariah.

Shariah-compliant hotels are shariah-compliant by design. An integral part of that compliance is the hotel architecture and functionality. Islamic architecture is a combination of Islamic design philosophy and Islamic principles from the Holy Quran and Sunnah. As a result, a shariah-compliant hotel is most feasible with a new facility designed by a team of experts to ensure shariah principles are entirely followed.

The hotel facility recognizes three zones: public space (lobby, reception, lounge), semi-private (restaurant, pool, gym, prayer room), and private (guest room). Food and beverage outlets in the hotel must be halal-certified by a halal certification body. Haram foods are prohibited from being brought in and consumed on the premises. During the holy month of Ramadan, pre-fasting meals and meals for the breaking of fast are served. Art, music, and entertainment should be shariah-compliant. Recreational facilities such as the swimming pool, health center, gym, and prayer room must be gender-specific. Religious facilities and services are available for congregational and Friday prayers. The hotel must adopt a shariah based financial system.

The hotel floor design in Shariah-compliant hotels have gender-based floor planning (female only floors) and family floors (families with children). The guest room design must have a clear indicator of the kiblah direction (which is checked by a religious authority), halal-certified toiletries and amenities, copy of the Holy Quran, prayer mats, and female prayer garments. Amongst others, the hotel room design must support washing (of part of the body) using water in preparation for formal prayers and reading the Holy Quran.

Muslim-friendly hotel

A Muslim-friendly hotel provides the needs of Muslim travelers, whereby halal products and services are available. A Muslim friendly hotel is feasible for both new and existing buildings.

Food and beverage outlets in the hotel must be halal-certified by a halal certification body or the hotel should have proper arrangements with a third-party halal-certified food service provider to cater to halal food. Recreational facilities must be gender-specific in place or in time. For example, in the morning the swimming pool is open for females and families only. The hotel should have a prayer room available for prayers.

The guest room design must have a clear indicator of the kiblah direction (which is checked by a religious authority), halal toiletries and amenities are available (or clearly marked non-halal in case non-halal), and prayer mats and female prayer garments are made available (upon request). When a room is allocated to Muslim guests, the room (including mini-bar) should not have any non-halal food and beverages.

Source: Jais 2017a, 2017b

of McDonald's far more easily than one from Nestlé. In case of unsatisfactory service, the angry customer can take a video of the encounter and upload this within minutes to social media. The facility, equipment, and tools should meet the highest standards of cleanliness (hygiene), quality, and halal as it is personally inspected by the customer in every encounter

As for services, 'operations' is involved in the actual marketing and promotion, any compromises in customer contact, systems and operational routines, and halal assets damages customer experience and customer delight. This makes the concept of halal excellence most essential for any services organisation.

Marketing mistakes

Marketing and sales are primary activities in the halal value chain. Marketing determines the relationship with the Muslim consumer through communication at various levels. Halal has implications for marketing decisions that require serious attention by organisations. Marketing mistakes are easily made and the consequences are far-reaching. What are some marketing mistakes practised by companies operating in and exporting to Islamic countries?

Marketing mistakes to avoid:

- **Marketing not involved in a halal certification programme:** Halal certification programmes are often considered just a product and/or market compliance project, involving people mainly from production, purchasing, and quality. The role of marketing, if at all, is often limited. This is incorrect, as marketing touches on various important areas during a halal certification programme and has major influences for effective halal issues and reputation management
- **Marketing team not trained on halal:** In big organisations, marketing is not based in the factory, but at the head office. Although the factory personnel are trained on halal, they

forget about the marketing department located in the national, regional, or global head office. Mistakes by marketing can have severe consequences on sales and corporate reputation
- **Sales story:** In communicating and promoting the value of products and services, marketing develops and communicates stories. Avoid any negative (*read*: non-halal) associations with the past. For example, this product used to have alcohol, used to be made with pork meat, was invented in a casino, etc
- **Product names and symbols:** There is such a thing as a 'non-halal product name' that cannot be used for halal products and services. For example, names with pig/pork, dog, champagne, beer, wine, casino (gambling), etc. Religious symbols and religious figures from Islam as well as other religions should not be used
- **Product image positioning:** Look, feel, and character of the product image should be halal. Imitating the look, feel, and character of something non-halal (like bacon, beer, casino), pushes the product into a grey area that can easily receive negative reactions in Muslim markets. Certain halal certification bodies will not be able to certify these products or might withdraw your halal certificate due to a new fatwa (religious ruling) or new halal standard
- **Sales promotion:** The context (location) of a promotion, clothes of promoters, behaviour of sales people, and co-packed products should be halal positive or halal neutral. A sales promotion of a halal product at a casino, promoted by a scarcely dressed lady, where together with your purchase you receive a free piggy bank should be avoided
- **Advertisement:** Advertisements communicate the image of the product and beyond. Ensure that the image being promoted is either supporting Islamic values or halal

neutral. Avoid scenes of other religions (like a Church or Temple), bars, casinos, pig farms, etc.
- **Not leveraging Muslim celebration:** The Islamic calendar has several important events during the year: Islamic New Year, Festival of Sacrifice (Eid Al-Adha), fasting month (Ramadan and Eid Al-Fitr), and the Prophet's birthday. In the same way that Nestlé is doing very well in Malaysia, you should use these events to associate a religious celebration with your brand to strengthen your corporate halal image. Muslim celebrations also provide an opportunity to create new products, flavours, or fragrances that pay respect to old Muslim traditions
- **Creating products on the edge of halal and non-halal:** Creating products that are on the edge of halal and non-halal are risky and if these are under consideration, need to be designed by halal experts. Some examples in this space are: chicken ham, beef bacon, non-alcoholic champagne, halal adult store, halal cryptocurrency, and halal sports betting

I would like to emphasise again that halal is founded on the religion of Islam, which is a sensitive matter for Muslims all over the world. Marketing and sales are primary activities in the halal value chain, of equal importance to operations and logistics, which must be robust by design. Halal expertise is needed in building and protecting your brand in Muslim markets.

Summary – chapter 8: Halal marketing

- Halal marketing covers those activities undertaken by an organisation in identifying and meeting the needs of the (Muslim) consumer. For halal marketing, high-touch engagements with the Muslim consumer are essential for halal trust

- Measuring marketing channel performance triggers possible modifications in (1) category offered in marketing channel; (2) channel partners; and (3) marketing channel design
- Services marketing is different from product marketing. In service delivery, customer contact, system and operational routines, and halal assets are key building blocks in halal services marketing
- Marketing and sales are primary activities in the halal value chain, of equal importance to operations and logistics, which needs to be robust by design. As marketing mistakes are costly, halal expertise is needed in building and protecting your brand in Muslim markets

Reflection questions

- What is the level of connectivity with Muslim societies in Muslim markets?
- What are the performance of my halal marketing channels?
- Is the marketing and promotion of my halal products halal positive, halal neutral, or halal negative?

References

Gronroos, C., 2007. *Service Management and: Customer Management in Service Competition marketing*, Third ed. John Wiley & Sons Ltd, Chichester.

Jais, A.S., 2017a. *Shariah Compliance & Accommodations: Concepts, Design & Guidelineshotels*. Politeknik Merlimau Melaka, Malacca.

Jais, A.S., 2017b. *Muslim-Friendly Services (MFHS) Management System: For Lodging and Accommodations Sectors Hospitality*. Politeknik Merlimau Melaka, Malacca.

Kester, R., 2000. *Channel Management: Ingrijpende Aanpassingen van Distributiekanalen op Komst. Samsom*, Alphen aan den Rijn (in Dutch).

Kotler, P., Kartajaya, H., Setiawan, I., 2017. *Marketing 4.0: Moving from Traditional to Digital*. John Wiley & Sons, New Jersey.

Lamelas, J.S., 2016. *Marketing: The Heart and the Brain of Branding*. LID Publishing Limited, Croydon.

Leboff, G., 2020. *Myths of Marketing: Banish the Misconceptions and Become a Great Marketer*. Kogan Page, London.

Porter, M.E., 1985. *Competitive Advantage: Creating and Sustaining Superior Performance*. The Free Press, New York.

PART IV

HALAL RISK AND REPUTATION MANAGEMENT

9

HALAL RISK MANAGEMENT

Gaps in halal risk management

Halal risk management practices of most companies are passive, meaning it is limited to the compliance of suppliers and their (manufacturing) operations based on the requirements of the Halal Certification Body (HCB) and their halal standard(s). On the other hand, halal risks in the entire supply chain are not on their radar screen. It is assumed by many organisations that the halal assurance system (HAS) and existing risk management practices provide sufficient support to handle halal incidents. This is a dangerous strategy for halal risk and reputation management.

Weaknesses in halal risk management can have severe consequences for both sales and corporate reputation as experienced by several large companies over the past years.

From my work as an advisor to the private sector ten common gaps can be found in halal risk management:

- Other than in the factory, employees in other corporate departments and of key supply chain partners are not trained on halal
- The halal status of cargo is not communicated on freight documents, cargo labels, and in IT systems throughout the supply chain, resulting in the mixing of halal with non-halal products in the transport and storage
- The halal status of cargo is not a consolidation criterion in the stuffing of less-than-container load (LCL) sea containers for ocean freight; less-than-truckload (LTL) for land transport; and unit load devices (ULD) or air cargo pallets for airfreight shipments. This results in the mixing of halal with non-halal products in transport
- The halal status of cargo is not a storage criterion in warehousing; resulting in the mixing of halal with non-halal products in storage
- Halal SOPs are not defined outside the factory operations in functions such as purchasing, marketing and sales, and logistics by the organisation and its supply chain partners (logistics service providers, distributors, and retailers). This directly affects the sustainability of the halal assurance system (HAS)
- Halal requirements are not covered in contracts with supply chain partners, other than suppliers of halal-certified ingredients and additives. Therefore, halal is often mixed with non-halal products by suppliers, logistics service providers, and distributors

- There is no halal risk mitigation and communication plan and halal risk recovery and communication plan, and there is no practise and repetition of halal incidents within the organisation and jointly with supply chain partners
- The crisis manual of corporations does not cover halal incidents at all, treats halal as a cross-contamination issue, or has a halal section that is not correct, consistent, complete, or clear
- The service industry, such as logistics service providers, distributors, and retailers are not well prepared for halal issue and crisis management; endangering the effectiveness of halal risk mitigation measures by the brand owner
- Vertical collaboration within supply chains and horizontal collaboration with other supply chains are not being practised, making risk management measures less effective by the brand owner

In short, risk management practices by brand owners and their supply chain is found to have serious gaps, resulting in a defective halal assurance system and halal risk management. Companies and supply chain partners are not well prepared for halal incidents. This exposes brands to high impact integrity violations and damages to sales and corporate reputation.

Halal risk management control

It is critical for both the Muslim consumer and the brand owner to better protect halal integrity along the supply chain. Halal, kosher, organic, GMO-free are known as credence quality attributed products, meaning that the characteristics of the product cannot be evaluated or ascertained by the individual consumer. As a result, halal risk management of products is essential for trust in halal-certified brands.

Halal integrity refers to the condition of the product being unquestionably halal. Whereas some halal integrity issues can be traced back to issues in slaughtering, manufacturing or processing, and packaging; a halal supply chain approach assumes that halal integrity issues can arise at any location throughout the supply chain. Managing halal integrity involves adopting proactive and reactive strategies to minimising the likelihood of delivering a compromised halal product and avoiding costly product recalls, crisis management, and business recovery.

Halal (supply chain) security refers to the prevention of contamination and doubt in halal products. Halal security problems can result from the actions and inactions of parties in each step of the supply chain from the source, where the product is halal certified, to the point of consumer purchase, where the final consumer receives the halal product. As discussed in chapter 3, contamination or doubt is created by (1) cross-contamination (breakage of packaging or improper packaging); (2) risk of contamination (failure to physically segregate between halal and non-halal, and lack of identification of halal cargo); and (3) misalignment with the perception of the Muslim consumer (based on the Islamic school of thought, fatwas, and local customs of the destination market). Halal supply chain security should, therefore, be treated as a core competence for a competitive advantage of a brand.

Halal security measures are put in place to protect the halal supply chain against risks, including intentional events. These security measures should defend against such risks and may prevent (or minimise the negative impact of) these risks from occurring, thereby increasing halal supply chain robustness. Building a robust halal supply chain should be a strategic initiative that changes the way halal supply chains are organised. In case of an incident, resilience is required in acting fast to isolate the halal issue, communicating the right message, and protecting the reputation of the company. Resilience is the ability of a system to return to its original state or move to a new, more desirable state after a halal incident. Therefore, next to robustness, resilience will be important in halal risk management.

Both proactive and reactive strategies are required for effective halal risk management, where robustness has a strong positive effect on performance; and resilience on customer value, brand, and corporate reputation. Although the halal assurance system (HAS) is an important basis, it requires additional building blocks in order to address halal risk management effectively. Figure 9.1 shows the components of halal risk management control. The following section will detail the halal risk management control components.

Halal supply chain risk prevention-mitigation-recovery cycles

Prevention

Contemporary supply chain strategies have increased the complexity and vulnerability of halal supply chains. This results

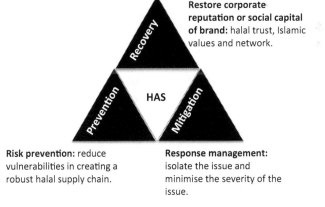

Figure 9.1 Halal risk management control.

in long supply chains, reduction of supplier base, global sourcing, centralised production, outsourcing, and centralised distribution, and low inventory levels in supply chains. Securing the supply chain takes a full understanding of your end-to-end supply chain and your position in the chain. As discussed in chapter 3, factors that affect halal supply chain vulnerability are product characteristics and market requirements. Bulk products are more vulnerable than unitised products, and cool chains are more vulnerable than dry (ambient) chains. Muslim-majority markets require halal assurance to address cross-contamination, risk of contamination, and the perception of the Muslim consumer; whereas for non-Muslim markets, halal assurance needs to address cross-contamination and risk of contamination only.

But what can be done to reduce halal supply chain vulnerabilities? The prevention or ex-ante controls are operationalised through the halal supply chain risk prevention cycle as shown in figure 9.2. The halal supply chain risk prevention cycle consists of four distinctive building blocks:

1. Risk vulnerability assessment
   A risk vulnerability assessment identifies possible halal issues in terms of chance and consequences. A risk vulnerability assessment answers three key questions (Sheffi and Rice 2005): 'What can go wrong? What is the likelihood of that happening? What are the consequences if it does happen?' The risk vulnerability assessment is a good starting point for building a robust halal supply chain design.

2. Supply chain (re)design
   As discussed in chapter 3, based on the product characteristics and market requirements, the parameters of the Halal Supply Chain Model (figure 3.4) are logistics

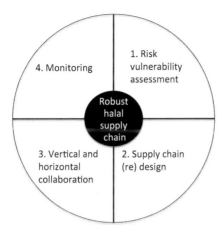

Figure 9.2 Halal supply chain risk prevention cycle.

control, supply chain resources, supply chain business processes, supply chain network structure, and performance indicators. A robust halal supply chain by design is based on the principles of the Halal Supply Chain Model.

Vulnerability is reduced through simplifying the supply chain structure and establishing halal control points and control measures in the halal supply chain. Vulnerability can be avoided in (parts of) the supply chain by having dedicated halal logistics assets: a dedicated halal warehouse and/or designated transport, or through containerisation at a lower level through for example a halal cargo box.

3. Vertical and horizontal collaboration

   As discussed in chapter 3, vertical and horizontal collaboration could provide beneficial strategies to better control of halal supply chains. Vertical and horizontal collaboration provide synergy advantages, essential for optimising halal supply chains.

4. Monitoring

    Monitoring is achieved by measuring halal supply performance through key performance indicators as well as conducting regular physical halal supply chain audits.

    A halal supply chain audit will verify the compliance of the supply chain operations with the requirements of the Halal Assurance System (HAS): has it been implemented properly and is it still correct-consistent-complete-clear? This audit can be conducted internally, by the internal halal auditor, or by another department that conducts other supply chain audits (e.g. purchasing or quality department). A third possibility is that a halal supply chain audit is conducted externally by a specialised auditing or consulting firm. The advantage of outsourcing audits to an independent party is that the company will be exposed to best practices and creating a fast-track learning curve, which results in a more robust halal supply chain.

Mitigation

Important principles in mitigation are control, coherence, and coordination. It is essential to be in full control of the halal supply chain during a halal incident. Supply chain processes and capabilities are key enablers for effective control with a halal issue. Coherence of the supply chain, holding it together to form a whole, is pivotal during halal incidents that might put a lot of pressure on the company, supply chain partners, and its staff. Coherence is enhanced through meaning, direction, and understanding during the worst times of the halal incident. In terms of coordination, three levels can be identified, namely organisation level (coordination among key departments); the halal supply chain (coordination among key supply chain partners); and external stakeholders (coordination with HCB, Muslim associations, government authorities, media, etc.).

Mitigation or in-process controls are the response management to isolate the halal issue and minimise the severity of the issue on the integrity of the halal supply chain. These are operationalised through the halal supply chain risk mitigation cycle (figure 9.3). The halal supply chain risk mitigation cycle consists of four distinctive building blocks:

1. Investigative audits
   Investigative audits are used for halal incidents to determine first if the issue is a halal issue or not. The internal halal auditor conducts the diagnosis of a halal issue, and advises the most suitable cause of action to solving the halal issue. The investigative audit is led by the internal halal auditor of the brand owner and reported to the halal committee chairman.

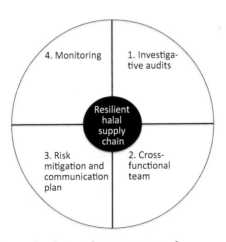

Figure 9.3 Halal supply chain risk mitigation cycle.

2. Cross-functional team

   A cross-functional team is formed and will be in charge during the mitigation exercise to make corporate decisions on the halal issue. This team consists of representatives from the halal committee (at least the chairman and internal halal auditor), purchasing, production, logistics, marketing and sales, quality department, corporate communication, and possible other relevant departments. The cross-functional team assures visibility of the halal supply chain concerned and allows for speed in decision making. Speed is essential in isolating and solving a halal issue, and avoiding escalation of the issue into a halal crisis.

3. Risk mitigation and communication plan

   The risk mitigation and communication plan is implemented by the cross-functional team to ensure fast response. Evidently, the path to fast mitigation involves effective process management and communications across their own organisation, the supply chain, and relevant external stakeholders. This plan, therefore, needs solid practise and repetition by the company and key supply chain partners (the so-called managed process links).

4. Monitoring

   Through monitoring of the halal issue, the supply chain concerned, and halal performance the cross-functional mitigation team is fed with information to make the best decisions possible as performance monitoring is needed during a halal incident. This requires incorporating a performance dashboard in the risk mitigation and communication plan. When the halal issue is resolved, the risk mitigation and communication plan is reviewed if further enhancements can be made to this corporate document.

Recovery

The main objective of recovery is to restore the corporate reputation or social capital of the brand, namely its (1) halal trust; (2) Islamic values; and (3) network.

Halal trust requires a public reconfirmation from the halal certification body that the product is halal. This is an important statement, which needs to be communicated extensively by the brand owner. But this not always easy to obtain quickly, as the HCB requires its own thorough investigation on the halal incident. The company should therefore not depend on this statement, but instead take full responsibility in steering the recovery process.

Islamic values need to be reemphasised by the brand owner through deeds in unison with the relevant religious school of thought, fatwas and local customs, which need to be communicated (*read*: shared) extensively by the brand owner.

Third, the halal supply chain network might have been affected by the halal incident, or may require adjustments when the cause of the halal crisis (a supply chain partner or employee) is removed from the supply chain or organisation.

You will need the best team to get through this and emerge from a halal crisis with the least damages. Support from halal experts in this process is priceless during a recovery exercise in minimising your sales backslash and corporate reputation damages.

Recovery or ex-post controls are operationalised during a halal crisis by a halal supply chain risk recovery cycle as shown in figure 9.4. A cross-functional team leads the risk recovery exercise, which is in principle the same team as the cross-functional risk mitigation team. It is recommended, however, to strengthen this team with an external halal advisor to better navigate through these unchartered waters.

HALAL RISK AND REPUTATION MANAGEMENT

Figure 9.4 Halal supply chain risk recovery cycle.

The halal supply chain risk recovery cycle consists of four distinctive building blocks:

1. Risk recovery and communication plan
   The implementation of a risk recovery and communication plan allows to act swiftly during a halal crisis. The risk recovery and communication plan needs practise and repetition by the company and key supply chain partners (the so-called managed process links).
2. Resume operations
   Resuming operations might need additional resources to get back on track. Vertical and horizontal collaboration during recovery helps in mobilising these resources (e.g. ingredients, equipment, people, logistics, etc.) and complementary skills in the supply chain in the most effective way.
3. Maintain employee support
   Maintaining employee support during a halal crisis is not always easy as halal is part of religion and employees might be

personally attacked for working for a company involved in a halal incident. For continuity of operations and resilience, a lot of attention needs to be paid to secure employee commitment during these difficult times. Next to good leadership, research shows that employee commitment is only possible if risk awareness is already present throughout the organisation and its key supply chain partners (the so-called managed process links).

4. Review risk mitigation and recovery plan

    A crisis is an enormously painful and expensive learning curve, which experiences obtained should not go to waste. Therefore, first review the effectiveness of the risk mitigation and recovery plans for managing a halal issue and halal crisis. Second, the halal crisis should provide recommendations to strengthen halal supply chain risk prevention, in particular the risk vulnerability assessment, supply chain (re)design, vertical and horizontal collaboration, and supply chain monitoring.

The halal supply chain prevention, mitigation and recovery cycles discussed provide proactive and reactive strategies for effective halal risk management control that ensure both robust and resilient halal supply chains. This needs a correct-consistent-complete-clear design, practise, and repetition by the company and its key supply chain partners.

Halal supply chain risk profile

Halal risk management should be rational and vary according to the halal supply chain risk profile, resulting in different halal risk intensity for different supply chain scenarios.

The halal supply chain risk profile of a company is determined by the following parameters (Tieman 2017):

- Food products require more extensive risk management than non-food products
- Products that are animal-based require more extensive risk management than products that are non-animal based
- Suppliers from non-Muslim countries require more extensive risk management than suppliers from predominantly Muslim countries
- Logistics service providers and distributors involved in distribution to Muslim-majority countries require more extensive risk management than for non-Muslim countries
- Brands from non-Muslim countries require more extensive risk management than brands from predominantly Muslim countries

These parameters are vital for a solid and cost-effective design of your halal risk management control.

Summary – chapter 9: Halal risk management

- Halal risk management practices of most companies are passive and show serious gaps, resulting in a defective halal assurance system and halal risk management
- For effective risk management control of a halal incident, a halal assurance system (HAS) and conventional risk management practices are not sufficient
- The halal supply chain risk prevention, mitigation, and recovery cycles create proactive and reactive strategies for effective halal risk management control that ensure both robust and resilient halal supply chains
- Halal risk management should be rationalised to vary according to the halal supply chain risk profile. This results in different halal risk intensity for different halal supply chain scenarios

Reflection questions

- What is your halal supply chain risk profile based on your halal supply chain scenarios?
- How to build a solid halal supply chain risk prevention for your company?
- What are the components of a risk mitigation and recovery plan for your organisation?

References

Sheffi, Y., Rice, J. B., Jr, 2005. A supply chain view of the resilient enterprise. MIT Sloan management review 47 (1), 40–48.

Tieman, M., 2017. Halal risk management: combining robustness and resilience. Journal of Islamic Marketing 8 (3), 461–475. https://doi.org/10.1108/JIMA-06-2015-0041.

10

HALAL REPUTATION MANAGEMENT

Halal reputation

A series of high-profile halal issues and scandals with top brands in recent years have shown that halal reputation and loyalty from the Muslim consumer can change very quickly. Through social media, a single halal issue can easily snowball into a major crisis for brand owners on a global scale, like in the case of Cadbury Malaysia (Halal Insight 10.1) in the year 2014. The Cadbury case clearly shows that companies need to understand that their brand and business can be at serious risk with a halal incident.

Halal Insight 10.1 Cadbury Malaysia

Cadbury, a Mondelez company, is a multinational confectionery company producing chocolates for Muslim markets, with one of its manufacturing plants located in Malaysia. Cadbury is certified by the Malaysian halal authority JAKIM. Malaysia's halal logo is considered one of the preferred halal logos to have on a product, acting as a pillar of trust for halal products and brands. The halal authority JAKIM has certified that all ingredients used and its production process meets Malaysia's stringent halal requirements and at the same time, a solid halal assurance system is in place.

In May 2014, a government officer from the Ministry of Health Malaysia leaked information about a possible porcine contamination with two Cadbury chocolate bars manufactured in Malaysia. This rumour went viral, resulting in a waterfall of negative messages on social media from Muslim consumers, Muslim associations, and Islamic non-government organisations (NGOs). After the leak, Cadbury's halal certificate for these two products was suspended for 17 days by JAKIM. Only ten days after the leak, based on a thorough investigation by the halal authority, JAKIM in a public statement confirmed that Cadbury products have no porcine DNA. During these ten days, the Muslim consumer was uncertain and confused about the halal status of these two Cadbury products. Although Cadbury took immediate action, such as a product recall of the two products, it affected not only the sales of Cadbury products in Malaysia but in many of its Muslim markets. The Cadbury issues also infected the entire Mondelez organisation and its brands.

This crisis, based on a rumour, resulted in unfortunate corporate reputation damages to a multinational company that takes halal very seriously. It is good to realise that such a crisis also had a major impact on Cadbury employees, both Muslims and non-Muslims. They have been working together

> since to recover from this crisis, and repair their corporate halal reputation and lost sales.
>
> *Source:* Musa et al. 2016, Tieman 2019

It seems that companies are under more continuous scrutiny than ever before. Major brand owners are concerned with their company's halal reputation. Unfortunately, companies only discover the actual value of their halal reputation (which they just lost) when they are involved in a halal crisis. Even though halal reputation may be hard to define and value, it is critical for businesses operating in Muslim markets to measure its performance.

What is the problem?

Muslims are less prepared to tolerate risks, whether real or perceived. It can be argued that Muslims want a near zero-risk halal environment. Furthermore, Muslims are intrinsically motivated to actively boycott brands that seem to be in violation of some of the teaching of Islam (Alserhan 2010, Ishak et al. 2018). As a result, the integrity of halal supply chains is becoming an increasing concern for industries and governments. Halal integrity issues are more likely to occur now with the fast-growing halal industry. Once detected, halal issues go viral on the internet, exposing not only the reputation of corporate brands but also a country's halal brand.

- Corporate halal reputation is vulnerable due to the way companies are organised
- Muslim markets are supplied by global supply networks of multinationals manufacturing their brands in different production locations with a different halal context, resulting in

complex global integrated halal supply chain networks and a coupling of brands

Coupling of brands occurs when producing different product brands from one production facility. For example, a multinational uses one production plant in Thailand to produce shampoos for the entire Asian marketing under different product brands. Second, companies practise co-branding at the product level (with a special ingredient added to a product), outlet level (for example Coca-Cola served in all McDonald's restaurants), and service level (our products are delivered by DHL). This kind of co-branding between different brands exposes a brand to correlation: when there is a halal crisis with one of the brands, it will affect the other brand as well. This occurs in spite of no technical evidence of the causality of a halal incident of one brand causing halal integrity issues with another brand.

There is a grand diversity in the awareness and adoption of the halal concept. At the same time, there is an evident increasing level of halal awareness among Muslim consumers. Halal issues in the supply chain, whether intentional or unintentional, can lead to a complete breakdown in consumer trust in a brand. The Muslim consumer of today has high demands and shares information quicker. Attitudes towards global brands have changed.

- In line with an integrative view of reputation management as described by Fombrun and Riel in their article 'The Reputational Landscape' (Fombrun and Riel 1997), I propose the following definition of halal reputation: 'A corporate halal reputation is a collective representation of the firm's past actions and halal performance, and the firm's future ability to meet halal requirements'

Corporate halal reputation not only considers the past performance, but also a future perspective to meeting future halal requirements. Various drivers contribute to the strength of a company's halal reputation. Those that are most influential are: halal authenticity; trustworthiness of halal certification body (HCB); messages by company and supply chain partners; and messages by external stakeholders. These drivers interact with each other and determine the corporate halal reputation.

Halal authenticity

Halal authenticity is the halal DNA of a company and the most valuable asset for corporate halal reputation. Amongst others, leading factors in halal authenticity are: the halal strategy of the company, degree of strategic alignment, and the halal maturity of the company. The halal strategy is a plan of action designed to achieve a long term or overall aim. The corporate halal strategy is made visible by its halal policy. The degree of strategic alignment, addressing both internal and external alignment to ensure a mutually rewarding relationship between the company and its key stakeholders enables a firm to meet its objectives and realise its purpose (Riel and Fombrun 2007, Riel 2012). Aligned organisations are more adaptive to evolving halal issues, more resilient in weathering halal crises, and establishing halal leadership. Third, how do we gauge an organisation's halal maturity (table 1.1)? In other words, the better the halal strategy, strategic alignment, and halal maturity, the higher the corporate halal reputation.

Trustworthiness of halal certification body (HCB)

HCBs are diverse and could either be from a business, non-government organisation, unit within a mosque, or a government department. As there are no international HCB guidelines and there is no global accreditation of HCBs available, there is a wide spectrum of HCBs available: ranging from absolutely opaque and untrustworthy, to highly transparent and trustworthy. An HCB from a Muslim-majority country, especially if government-linked, will have a higher perceived level of trust from the Muslim consumer than an HCB from a non-Muslim country. A higher reputation of HCB will influence the consumer perception regarding the product compliance with halal principles: its halal integrity. Therefore, HCBs could be ranked in order to quantify their trustworthiness. In other words, the better the reputation of an HCB, the higher the corporate halal reputation.

Messages by company and supply chain partners

Communication can be used to protect reputational assets during a crisis. Positive messages regarding the corporate halal reputation by companies and supply chain partners contribute to a positive corporate halal reputation, whereas negative messages by the company and its supply chain partners contribute negatively to the corporate halal reputation of a brand.

The response of a company within the supply chain is crafted by its corporate halal reputation strategy, and operationalised through its (or lack of) halal issue management and halal crisis management capabilities. Halal issue management capabilities require a solid risk mitigation and communication plan and execution through a cross-functional risk mitigation team. Halal crisis management is operationalised by a risk recovery and communication plan and executed through a cross-functional risk recovery team, which is the same team as the cross-functional risk mitigation team during a halal crisis. In other words: The more correct, consistent, complete, and clear the corporate halal reputation strategy, halal issue management, and halal crisis management, the higher the corporate halal reputation.

Messages by external stakeholders

Negative publicity about a halal incident becomes a threat to both the corporate reputation and sales of companies. Messages by external stakeholders are considered more trustworthy than messages from the company itself, are highly uncontrollable, and can go viral (Jahng and Hong 2017).

Key factors are: First, the level of connectivity with Muslim communities, ranging from mobile connectivity, experimental connectivity, and the ultimate level of social connectivity (Kotler et al. 2017, Kim and Krishna 2017). Is there an existing cooperation and trust-based relationship with Muslim communities (Heugens et al. 2004)? A second factor is the current company media coverage in relation to halal that can be found in newspapers, Google, Facebook, YouTube, Instagram, Twitter, etc. Third, what is the company track record with regards to halal issues and crises? How did the company handle a halal issue and crisis? What was the result and impact? In other words, the more advanced the connectivity with Muslim communities, the more positive the current media coverage and track record with halal issues and crises, the higher the corporate halal reputation.

Halal reputation drivers

As three out of four drivers are within the control of the company, brand owners to a large extent can be in control of their own halal reputation. However, this requires a measurement of your halal reputation drivers and taking control of these drivers. Halal scandals involving individual firms may cast a shadow over the entire industry, just as positive publicity may enhance the industry's halal reputation. Therefore, collective halal reputation management, all activities and behaviour undertaken by members of a collective to deliberately alter judgments about the reputation of the collective, should also be part of a corporate halal reputation strategy. Amongst others, collective halal reputation measures include initiatives such as halal knowledge sharing, joint halal research and development programmes, establishing an industry halal code of conduct, lobbying with halal authorities and Muslim consumer associations, and joint public relations and advertising initiatives.

Halal crisis

With a halal issue in Muslim markets, a whirlpool easily becomes a maelstrom, with a vortex dragging companies deep under. The lifebuoy thrown by corporate communication, based on their crisis manual, does not help companies to get out of this vortex but instead pulls companies further down towards the bottom of the ocean. As there is no lifeline attached to these lifebuoys, due to the many gaps in their halal risk management control, crisis manuals appear to be fake lifebuoys in times of a halal crisis.

A halal issue can be defined as a gap between the stakeholder's expected and perceived halal practices of a brand owner. The trigger of a halal crisis, a halal issue, can be classified as contamination, non-compliance, or perception issue. Table 10.1 presents a classification of halal issues with examples.

With a contamination issue, the Muslim consumer is uncertain if he or she has been 'poisoned' with haram (forbidden) ingredients in their food, cosmetics, pharmaceuticals, or other halal products purchased. Can he or she still trust the purity of the product and brand? Second, there could be non-compliance due to breakages in the halal supply chain, as well as issues with the halal certificate or halal logo. This scenario would make the halal status of the product doubtful, which Muslims, according to their religion, should avoid (Al-Qaradawi 2007). Third, it can also be perception related, where there is a possible mismatch

Table 10.1 Halal issue classification

1	**Contamination**	**Example**
a	Counterfeit product with halal logo	Counterfeit milk power with halal logo
b	Haram ingredient or contamination with haram	Claim of contamination of halal-certified chocolate with alcohol or pork
c	Poisonous ingredient in halal-certified product	Mercury in skin whitening cream which is halal certified
2	**Non-compliance**	**Example**
a	Expired halal certificate	Expired halal certificate of product, ingredient, or restaurant outlet
b	HCB of ingredient is not recognised anymore	On the recently updated list of recognised HCBs of Malaysia's halal authority JAKIM, a formerly recognised German HCB is removed from this list.
c	New fatwa making halal certified product haram	New fatwa (religious ruling) bans certain slaughtering methods
d	Non-compliance in logistics	Mixing of halal-certified product with beer/pork products in logistics or curtain sider with beer/pork/sexy lady
e	Fake or wrong halal logo on product or outlet	In Europe fake halal logos are used on products and restaurants as there is no law against it
f	Fake halal certificate	The manufacturer or restaurant carries a fake halal certificate
3	**Perception**	**Example**
a	Wrong commercial/advertising	Sexy dressed lady in commercial
b	Wrong promotion/co-packing	Piggybank or product containing alcohol co-packed with halal-certified product
c	Brand image of company is not positive	Company is boycotted because it is an American company
d	Halal authenticity is questioned of company	Company is involved in child labour, pollution, etc.
e	Halal issue that has been resolved already by HCB	A halal issue goes viral (again) which was already resolved a long time ago by the HCB

between perceived brand image and the Islamic way of life (Wilson and Liu 2011).

Although there are three different halal issue classifications and arguably different degrees of severity of a halal issue, the possible reputation consequences and damages can be in all three cases major if not handled well. As a result, there is a significant chance that a halal issue snowballs into a global halal crisis. A halal crisis is a situation where the corporate halal reputation is under attack, endangering the sales, and possibly even the existence of the company. This situation demands quick action from the brand owner to reduce reputation damages. Evidence from previous halal crises shows that the brand owner cannot fully rely on a quick response from halal authorities, leaving the brand owner in the main driving seat to address a halal crisis facing the company. Therefore, it is suggested that in order to better protect the brand and corporate halal reputation, a solid prevention, mitigation, and recovery system is built.

The same social media that provides a viral platform can also be used to serve as a vessel for authentic and transparent crisis communication. In halal crisis management, it is particularly important to share compassion and factual information. Social media allows for direct and unfiltered communication from the brand owner that according to Jahng and Hong (2017) is perceived as more credible than traditional media. Corporate halal reputation risks do not only affect individual organisations, but can affect an entire industry, requiring collective corporate halal reputation management strategies.

Despite realising the importance of corporate halal reputation, many organisations still continue to neglect corporate halal reputation risks and fail to track their halal reputation performance. The dynamics of the halal industry today and the emerging industry requirements, however, will make measuring the corporate halal reputation a critical success factor for doing business in Muslim markets.

The halal reputation index

Multinational companies today are measuring the halal image of the company by conducting a survey on the halal confidence in their brand. This measurement is just a contemporary view of the Muslim perception towards your brand, based on the image of a company in the past. Although you could argue that a halal image is important, it is not an accurate measure for companies to predict the corporate halal reputation in the future and is certainly not a key performance indicator for management to steer on. I would like to argue that measuring your halal image is like driving your Ferrari on the highway and just looking at your side mirrors. This sounds ok as long the road is straight, but by the first corner, you are out and will be crashing your car into a road divider or tree.

To address this, you need a more robust measurement for your corporate halal reputation. The Halal Reputation Index (HRI), developed by the LBB International Halal Research Centre, is a quantification of the halal reputation of a company or organisation based on an assessment of a number of factors, which drive and predict the corporate halal reputation of a company. HRI shown in figure 10.1 is based on an algorithm using four halal reputation drivers (halal authenticity; the trustworthiness of halal certification body; messages by company and supply chain partners; and messages by external stakeholders). The halal reputation index algorithm is based on ten main indicators (figure 10.2), supported by additional moderating and intervening variables.

HRI is the new key performance indicator for companies operating in Muslim markets, which acts as a predictor for corporate halal reputation and sales. The corporate halal reputation index requires a specific guardian, namely the chairman of the halal committee, but its performance tracked

HALAL REPUTATION MANAGEMENT 167

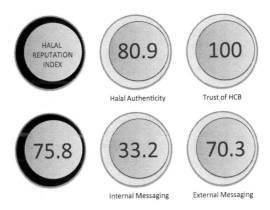

Figure 10.1 Halal reputation index.

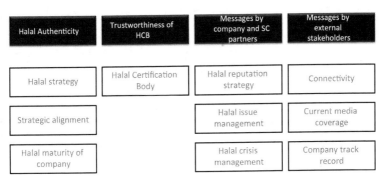

Figure 10.2 Halal reputation index indicators.

as a key performance indicator by top management. HRI measurement is also used for continuous improvement of the corporate halal assurance system and halal committee. In summary, the HRI becomes an essential measurement of achieving halal excellence. What gets measured gets accomplished.

Licence to operate rating

Companies serving Muslim markets need to earn their licence to operate. The key drivers for a licence to operate is the ability to anticipate halal market requirements, address them through a solid halal authenticity, a trustworthy halal certification body (HCB), the right messages by the company and supply chain partners, and positive messages by external stakeholders. This relationship is shown in figure 10.3. The halal market requirements are a critical denominator in the formula of the Licence to Operate rating in Muslim markets.

Although your overall corporate halal reputation (HRI) might be good, your Licence To Operate (LTO) rating might differ greatly per market. Changes in halal requirements (such as a new halal standard, new fatwa, or a new list in which halal certification bodies are recognised) can immediately change your LTO rating. Monitoring your LTO rating is a critical measurement for each Muslim-majority country your organisation is operating in or exporting to. Protecting your LTO in your Muslim markets requires internal and external alignment (Riel 2012).

Internal alignment within your own organisation and supply chain requires intelligence, information sharing, training, and monitoring. Intelligence is required regarding existing halal practices, halal awareness, and risk awareness within your own

Figure 10.3 Licence to operate rating.

organisation and supply chain partners. Gaps must be mapped and analysed. Inform staff and supply chain partners about the corporate halal strategy, its intent (niyyah), and implication for their operations. Training enables the company's staff and supply chain partner's staff in developing the right skills and ensuring consistent halal practices within the (end-to-end) supply chain. Facilitate risk awareness among your supply chain partners. Monitoring is necessary to track the progress of alignment and adjust where needed. Halal audits are, thus, not only important within the organisation but throughout the supply chain.

External alignment with external stakeholders requires market intelligence and a mix of strategies and tactics to achieve total stakeholder support. Emerging halal market requirements and in particular changes to the halal eco-system of a country, public opinion on addressing Islamic values by public and private organisations, and expected changes in halal standards must be monitored. This intelligence can be complemented by the benchmarking of corporate halal reputation with competitors. Hence, the systematic scanning of the halal market requirements is important for brand owners in order to identify gaps between the (emerging) market requirements and brand practices, and pro-actively addressing them in order to ensure sustainable high sales of brands operating in Muslim markets.

External alignment strategies and tactics involve informing the (Muslim) consumer, lobbying with halal certification bodies and Muslim consumer associations, hosting advocacy activities with the media, taking part in halal forums and conferences, participating in halal industry research, obtaining membership in influential think tanks and societies, and applying horizontal collaboration.

Halal reputation is a journey, starting with regarding halal reputation management as a problem to be addressed urgently, viewing halal reputation as an asset, considering halal reputation

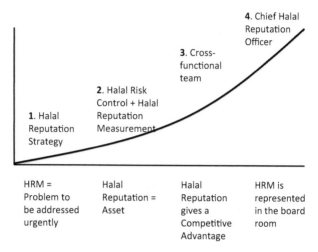

Figure 10.4 Halal reputation journey.

as a competitive advantage that can increase sales, and representing halal reputation management in the boardroom (figure 10.4). Setting halal reputation objectives by top management, related to the halal reputation journey, is an essential ingredient for halal reputation excellence.

Summary – chapter 10: Halal reputation management

- A corporate halal reputation is a collective representation of the firm's past actions and halal performance, and the firm's future ability to meet halal requirements. Halal reputation management is different from conventional corporate reputation management
- Drivers of a company's halal reputation are halal authenticity; the trustworthiness of halal certification body; messages by

company and supply chain partners; and messages by external stakeholders
- The trigger of a halal crisis, a halal issue, can be classified as contamination, non-compliance, or perception issue. Halal scandals involving individual firms may cast an entire industry into a bad light. Therefore, organisation should have both individual and collective corporate halal reputation management strategies
- The Halal Reputation Index (HRI) should be measured and included in balanced scorecards by top management. Halal authenticity, choice of HCB, internal messaging, and external messaging need to be aligned with the halal market requirements. An imbalance with the halal market requirements, defined in the Licence To Operate (LTO) rating, directly affects sales in Muslim markets

Reflection questions

- What is the corporate halal reputation of my company?
- How can I improve my Halal Reputation Index (HRI) and Licence To Operate (LTO) rating in my key Muslim markets?
- What are your corporate halal reputation objectives for the coming three years?

References

Al-Qaradawi, Y., 2007. *The Lawful and the Prohibited in Islam*. Islamic Book Trust, Petaling Jaya.

Alserhan, B. A., 2010. On Islamic branding: brands as good deeds. *Journal of Islamic Marketing* 1 (2), 101–106. https://doi.org/10.1108/17590831011055842.

Fombrun, C. J., Riel, C. B. Van, 1997. The reputational landscape. *Corporate Reputation Review* 1 (2), 5–13.

Heugens, P. P., Riel, C., Van, van den Bosch, F. A., 2004. Reputation management capabilities as decision rules. *Journal of Management Studies* 41 (8), 1349–1377. https://doi.org/10.1111/j.1467-6486.2004.00478.x.

Ishak, S., Khalid, K., Sulaiman, N., 2018. Influencing consumer boycott: between sympathy and pragmatic. *Journal of Islamic Marketing* 9 (1), 19–35. https://doi.org/10.1108/JIMA-05-2016-0042.

Jahng, M. R., Hong, S., 2017. How should you tweet?: The effect of crisis response voices, strategy, and prior brand attitude in social media crisis communication. *Corporate Reputation Review* 20 (2), 147–157.

Kim, S., Krishna, A., 2017. Bridging strategy versus buffering strategy: enhancing crisis management capability in public management for relational and reputational improvement, and conflict avoidance. *Asian Journal of Communication* 27 (5), 517–535. https://doi.org/10.1080/01292986.2017.1313876.

Kotler, P., Kartajaya, H., Setiawan, I., 2017. *Marketing 4.0: Moving from Traditional to Digital*. John Wiley & Sons, New Jersey.

Musa, N., Muslim, N., Omar, M. F. C., Husin, A., 2016. The Cadbury controversy: blessings in disguise? In: Manan, S.K.A., Rahman, F.A., Shri, M. (Eds.), *Contemporary Issues and Development in the Global Halal Industry*. Springer, Singapore, 95–104. https://doi.org/10.1007/978-981-10-1452-9_9.

Riel, C. Van, Fombrun, C. J., 2007. *Essentials of Corporate Communication: Implementing Practices for Effective Reputation Management*. Routledge, Oxon.

Riel, C. Van, 2012. *The Alignment Factor: Leveraging the Power of Total Stakeholder Support*. Routledge, Oxon.

Tieman, M., 2019. Measuring corporate halal reputation: a corporate halal reputation index and research propositions. *Journal of Islamic Marketing* 11 (3), 591–601. https://doi.org/10.1108/JIMA-05-2018-0095.

Wilson, J. A. J., Liu, J., 2011. The challenges of Islamic branding: navigating emotions and halal. *Journal of Islamic Marketing* 2 (1), 28–42. https://doi.org/10.1108/17590831111115222.

EPILOGUE: A PURSUIT OF EXCELLENCE

This book shares the building blocks of professional halal business management. Halal business management starts with the first step: the intention of establishing halal excellence. It is good to realise that halal excellence is not an end state. Halal excellence is a process, a pursuit of excellence. This book presented best practices in halal business management, covering halal certification, halal supply chain management, halal branding and marketing, and halal risk and reputation management.

Halal certification

Not only is the halal industry a fast-growing market due to demographics, the halal industry is also expanding in both width (more product categories can be halal-certified) and depth (more companies are embracing halal certification). Both Muslim and non-Muslim countries serve halal markets. However, halal certification of products, outlets, and services is an essential requirement for doing business in Muslim markets.

The foundation of a halal assurance system is your quality management system. The halal assurance system is a module on top of your quality management system, and does not replace your quality management system. The design of your halal assurance system is crucial as it should be compliant with halal requirements, able to meet emerging requirements, and ensure practical operations serving both Muslim-majority and non-Muslim countries. A halal certification programme typically consists of four steps: halal strategy, 0-base assessment, halal assurance system documentation, and implementation.

Halal supply chain management

Halal is not static, but is going through an evolution from a product approach towards a supply chain and halal value approach. The halal integrity of a product is a function of the supply chain. The halal integrity is a strong as its weakest link, not its strongest link. The Halal Supply Chain Model is introduced as a management model to design and manage halal supply chains.

Halal business management has major implications for the purchasing function. The purchasing department needs to adjust its procurement strategy and purchasing processes to ensure sustainable halal purchasing and operations for the company. Most companies outsource their logistics and supply chain activities and processes to logistics service providers. When you outsource these activities or processes, the brand owner is still responsible for the halal integrity of its supply chain network. Evidence supports that engaging a logistics service provider that is halal-certified strengthens your halal risk management. The retailer completes an end-to-end halal supply chain, where the halal product is handed over to the consumer upon payment. The development of halal clusters allows for better organisation and upscaling of halal production, which is highly necessary to alleviate bottlenecks in supply and to support the fast growth of the halal industry. Halal parks and halal zones can create a superior halal eco-system for companies to operate in, simplifies halal, and harvest synergy advantages.

Halal branding and marketing

The goal of branding a product halal is to communicate to the consumer that the product has been verified halal by an independent halal certification body. There are three possible ways to communicate this, through halal co-branding, halal ingredient branding, and halal-coding. Branding halal is purely a branding and marketing decision, whereas having halal certification is entirely a risk management decision.

Building a strong brand in Muslim markets requires careful planning and long-term investment, and is the result of an ongoing, steady stream of consistent small efforts, not a series of one-off, gigantic pushes. Halal brand equity is the added Islamic values endowed to products and services. There are three halal brand equity asset classifications defined: halal commodity, potential halal asset, and acquired halal asset. The positioning of a brand is about crafting a corporate image to occupy a distinctive place in the mind of the target market. A halal brand positioning matrix has been introduced, based on two dimensions: (1) 'Does the brand originate from an Islamic country or non-Islamic country?'; (2) 'Does the brand owner position the brand as a halal brand or halal product (or service)?'

Halal marketing covers those activities undertaken by an organisation to identify and meet the needs of the Muslim consumer. Market segmentation, value chain and value network, and marketing channels are core marketing concepts that are relevant for halal marketing. Customer contact, system and operational routines, and the halal assets are key building blocks in halal services marketing. Marketing and sales are primary activities in the halal value chain, of equal importance to operations and logistics, which must be robust by design. As marketing mistakes are costly, halal expertise is needed in building and protecting your brand in Muslim markets.

Halal risk and reputation management

Current halal risk management practices of most companies are passive and show serious gaps, resulting in a defective halal assurance system and poor halal risk management. For effective risk management control of a halal incident, a halal assurance system and conventional risk management practices are not sufficient. The halal supply chain risk prevention, mitigation, and recovery cycles create proactive and reactive strategies for effective risk management control that ensures both robust and resilient halal supply chains.

Halal reputation management is different from conventional corporate reputation management. Halal reputation has been defined as a collective representation of the firm's past actions and halal performance, and the firm's ability to meet future halal requirements. Measuring the corporate halal reputation is essential for companies to protect their corporate reputation and sales in Muslim markets. Companies need to earn their licence to operate and ensure the alignment of their halal authenticity, choice of halal certification body, internal messaging, and external messaging with their market requirements. The Halal Reputation Index (HRI) and Licence To Operate (LTO) rating have been introduced as key performance indicators for companies operating in and exporting to Muslim-majority countries. What gets measured, gets accomplished.

Are you ready for halal excellence?

The core purpose of halal excellence is the creation of products and services that are lawful and good. There are seven main principles introduced to embracing the halal excellence philosophy:

1. No compromises on inputs (ingredients, equipment, and people) and processes
2. Halal excellence by *design*
3. Practise and repetition of the halal assurance system, halal risk management control, and halal reputation management
4. Effective command and control of your halal supply chain and corporate halal reputation
5. Having the best team: your staff in your company, but also your supply chain partners, and external stakeholders
6. Engagement with your customer
7. In balance with nature (*mizan*)

Successful companies in the halal industry are those companies that embrace halal excellence by *design*. Halal excellence is a process - a pursuit of excellence. Halal business management is beyond halal certification, and needs to address also supply chain management, halal branding and marketing, and risk and reputation management. Finally, halal excellence needs measurement through the adoption of appropriate key performance indicators, to protect your halal reputation and licence to operate in Muslim markets.

Welcome to the halal industry and success in serving Muslim markets through halal excellence.

May peace be upon you.

Marco Tieman, PhD

APPENDIX 1

HALAL CERTIFICATION INFORMATION CHECKLIST

Use the checklist below to keep track of the information needed from both the organisation itself as well as your suppliers. Remember that the information from suppliers is on the critical path of any halal certification programme.

A. General

1. Company name
2. Parent company name
3. Name of products to be halal certified
4. Existing product certificates of these products (organic, kosher, etc.)

5. Type of products (retail/non-retail)
6. Organisation chart of plant
7. Company profile (vision and mission, policy, quality policy, etc.)
8. Company address (HQ and halal production site)
9. List of permits of production plant(s)
10. List of project committee for this project: name, telephone, email, mobile (XLS file)

B. Site information

1. Map of plant location, layout of relevant plant and layout of overall site complex
2. Quality system manuals and certificates (ISO, HACCP, etc.)
3. Flow chart of the production process of products to be halal certified
4. List of SKUs (stock-keeping units) to be halal certified
5. Sample of freight documents used (receiving and shipping)
6. Sample of cargo labels used on cargo (receiving and shipping)
7. Sample of product in primary packaging
8. Sample of carton boxes used
9. Sample of any special cargo bags/boxes used for airfreight, sea freight, etc. (if any)
10. Sample of contracts of:
    - Supplier
    - Logistics service provider, transporter, warehouse operator
    - Distributor
    - Customer

C. Product information for production plant

I. For each product:
   1. Raw material matrix for each product
   2. For each raw material:

1. Material name
2. Supplier name
3. Country of origin
4. Material flow chart (in case it is manufactured/processed, else list of ingredients)
5. Certificate of Analysis and other supporting documents (GMO, Organic, etc.)
6. Halal certificate (when available)

II. For each primary packaging material (bottle, can, etc.):
1. Material name
2. Supplier name
3. List of ingredients
4. Halal certificate (when available)

III. Process aids (e.g. water filter, soap to clean pipes and tanks, etc.)
1. Product name
2. Supplier name
3. List of ingredients
4. Halal certificate (when available)

NOTE: As every halal certification body has its own unique information submission requirements, please consult your halal certification body or halal advisor for a complete information request.

APPENDIX 2

HALAL BUSINESS MANAGEMENT EDUCATION

For universities and other professional education institutes interested in offering the subject Halal Business Management for bachelor, master programme, or executive courses, this book is an excellent coursebook. This book is also a suitable reader for industry workshops on halal business management and related topics.

Below is a possible module structure of a Halal Business Management course.

Lecture 1: Introduction to Halal
Book chapter 1: The World of Halal

Topics to cover:

- What is halal?
- The structure of the halal industry
- Control of halal chains
- Halal excellence philosophy

Recommended literature:

- Al-Qaradawi, Y. (2007). *The lawful and the prohibited in Islam.* Islamic Book Trust, Kuala Lumpur
- Evans, A., and Syed, S. (2015). *From Niche to Mainstream: Halal Goes Global.* International Trade Centre, Geneva
- Tieman, M. (2011). The application of Halal in supply chain management: in-depth interviews. *Journal of Islamic Marketing.* 2 (2), 186-195. DOI: https://doi.org/10.1108/17590831111139893
- Tieman, M. (2012). Control of halal food chains. *Islam and Civilisational Renewal.* 3 (3), 538-542
- Tieman, M., & Hassan, F. H. (2015). Convergence of food systems: Kosher, Christian and Halal. *British Food Journal.* 117 (9), 2317-2327. DOI: https://doi.org/10.1108/BFJ-02-2015-0058
- Tieman, M. (2016). Halal Diets. *Islam and Civilisational Renewal.* 7 (1), 128-132

Lecture 2: Halal Assurance System and Halal Certification

Book chapter 2: Halal Assurance System

Topics to cover:

- What is a halal assurance system?
- The halal certification body
- Local and international halal standards
- Steps in halal certification

Recommended literature:

- Shah, M.S.A.A. (2017). *Halal Certification: in the light of the Shari'ah*. Sanha Halal Associates Pakistan, Karachi.
- Tieman, M. (2011). The application of Halal in supply chain management: in-depth interviews. *Journal of Islamic Marketing*. Vol. 2 No. 2, pp. 186-195. DOI: https://doi.org/10.1108/17590831111139893
- Tieman, M., and Hassan, F. H. (2015). Convergence of food systems: Kosher, Christian and Halal. *British Food Journal*. Vol. 117 No. 9, pp. 2313-2327. DOI: https://doi.org/10.1108/BFJ-02-2015-0058
- Tieman, M. (2015). Halal Certification Procedures: Some Unresolved Issues. *Islam and Civilisational Renewal*. Vol. 6 No. 1, pp. 124-127
- Tieman, M. (2017). Halal Europe: A Premium Halal-Tayyib Brand? *Islam and Civilisational Renewal*. Vol. 8 No. 2, pp. 260-263
- Tieman, M., & Williams, G. (2019). Creative Destruction of Halal Certification (Bodies). *Islam and Civilisational Renewal* (ICR), Vol. 10 No. 1, pp. 127-131

- Your local halal standard (if any); International halal standard (SMIIC, in development)

Lecture 3: The Halal Supply Chain
Book chapter 3: The Halal Supply Chain

Topics to cover:

- Introduction to supply chain management
- Foundation of halal supply chain management
- The Halal Supply Chain model
- Synergy in halal supply chains
- Halal blockchains

Recommended literature:

- Tieman, M. (2011). *Halal SuperHighway*. GRIN Publishing GmbH, Munich
- Tieman, M., van der Vorst, J. G., and Ghazali, M. C. (2012). Principles in halal supply chain management. *Journal of Islamic Marketing*. Vol. 3 No. 3, pp. 217-243. DOI: https://doi.org/10.1108/17590831211259727
- Tieman, M. (2014). Synergy in halal supply chains. *Islam and Civilisational Renewal*. Vol. 5 No. 3, pp. 454-459
- Tieman, M., and Darun, M. R. (2017). Leveraging blockchain technology for halal supply chains. Islam and Civilisational Renewal. Vol. 8 No. 4, pp. 547-550
- Tieman, M., Darun, M. R., Fernando, Y., and Ngah, A. B. (2019). Utilizing Blockchain Technology to Enhance Halal Integrity: The Perspectives of Halal Certification Bodies. In *World Congress on Services*. Springer, Cham, pp. 119-128. DOI: https://doi.org/10.1007/978-3-030-23381-5_9

Lecture 4: Halal Purchasing
Book chapter 4: Halal Purchasing

Topics to cover:

- Introduction to purchasing
- Halal procurement maturity
- Halal procurement strategy
- Horizontal collaboration
- Halal purchasing process

Recommended literature:

- Kraljic, P. (1983). Purchasing must become supply management. *Harvard Business Review*. September/ October, Vol. 61 No. 5, pp. 109-117
- Tieman, M., and Ghazali, M. C. (2013). *Principles in halal purchasing*. Journal of Islamic Marketing. Vol. 3 No. 3, pp. 217-243. DOI: https://doi.org/10.1108/JIMA-01-2012-0004
- Weele, J. van (2002). *Purchasing and Supply Chain Management: Analysis, Planning and Practice*. Third Edition. Thomson, London

Lecture 5: Halal Logistics and Retailing
Book chapter 5: Halal Logistics and Retailing

Topics to cover:

- The halal logistics service provider
- Local and international halal logistics standards
- Halal warehouse
- Halal transport
- Halal compliant terminal

- Halal retailing

Recommended literature:

- Susanty, A., Caterina, A. D., Tieman, M., Hidayat, R. D. R., and Jati, S. (2019). Mapping the Drivers in Implementing Halal Logistic. In 2019 IEEE International Conference on Industrial Engineering and Engineering Management (IEEM). IEEE, pp. 253-257. DOI: https://doi.org/10.1109/IEEM44572.2019.8978628
- Tieman, M., van der Vorst, J. G., and Ghazali, M. C. (2012). Principles in halal supply chain management. Journal of Islamic Marketing. Vol. 3 No. 3, pp. 217-243. DOI: https://doi.org/10.1108/17590831211259727
- Tieman, M., Ghazali, M.C., and van der Vorst, J.G. (2013). Consumer perception on halal meat logistics. British Food Journal. Vol. 115 No. 8, pp. 1112-1129. DOI: https://doi.org/10.1108/BFJ-10/2011-0265
- Tieman, M. and van Nistelrooy, M. (2014). Perception of Malaysian food manufacturers towards halal logistics. Journal of International Food & Agribusiness Marketing. Vol. 26 No. 3, pp. 218-233. DOI: https://doi.org/10.1080/08974438.2013.833572
- Tieman, M. and Ghazali, M.C. (2014). Halal Control Activities and Assurance Activities in Halal Food Logistics. Procedia-Social and Behavioral Sciences. Vol. 121, pp. 44-57
- Tieman, M. and Ruiz-Bejarano, B. (2020). Halal Retailing: Closing the Last Mile in an End-to-end Halal Supply Chain. Islam and Civilisational Renewal. Vol. 11 No. 1, pp. 147-152
- Zailani, S., Kanapathy, K., Iranmanesh, M., and Tieman, M. (2015). Drivers of halal orientation strategy among halal food firms. British Food Journal. Vol. 117 No. 8, pp. 2143 – 2160. DOI: https://doi.org/10.1108/BFJ-01-2015-0027

- Your local halal logistics standard (if any); International Halal Supply Chain Management System standard (SMIIC, in development)

Lecture 6: Halal Clusters
Book chapter 6: Halal Clusters

Topics to cover:

- Introduction to clusters
- Halal clusters and the Halal Cluster Model
- Halal parks and halal zones

Recommended literature:

- Tieman, M. (2015). Halal clusters. *Journal of Islamic Marketing*. Vol. 6 No. 1, pp. 2-21. DOI: https://doi.org/10.1108/JIMA-05-2014-0034

Lecture 7: Halal Branding
Book chapter 7: Halal Branding

Topics to cover:

- Halal trust
- Branding halal
- Halal brand equity assets
- Halal brand positioning

Recommended literature:

- Alserhan, B. A. (2010). On Islamic branding: brands as good deeds. *Journal of Islamic Marketing*. Vol. 1 No. 2, pp. 101-106. DOI: https://doi.org/10.1108/17590831011055842

- Tieman, M. (2019). Branding Halal: A Delicate Balance. *Islam and Civilisational Renewal* (ICR). Vol 10 No. 2, pp. 283-287
- Wilson, J.A.J. (2018). *Halal Branding*. Claritas Books, Swansea

Lecture 8: Halal Marketing
Book chapter 8: Halal Marketing

Topics to cover:

- Halal Marketing Strategy
- Halal Services Marketing
- Marketing Mistakes

Recommended literature:

- Alserhan, B.A. (2016). *The principles of Islamic marketing*. Second Edition. Routledge, Oxon
- Temporal, P. (2011). *Islamic Branding and Marketing: creating a global Islamic business*. John Wiley & Sons, Singapore
- Wilson, J.A.J. (2018). *Halal Branding*. Claritas Books, Swansea

Lecture 9: Halal Risk Management
Book chapter 9: Halal Risk Management

Topics to cover:

- Gaps in halal risk management
- Halal risk management control
- The halal supply chain risk prevention-mitigation-recovery cycles

- Halal supply chain risk profile

Recommended literature:

- Tieman, M. (2017). Halal risk management: combining robustness and resilience. *Journal of Islamic Marketing*. Vol. 8 No. 3, pp. 461-475 DOI: https://doi.org/10.1108/JIMA-06-2015-0041

Lecture 10: Halal Reputation Management
Book chapter 10: Halal Reputation Management

Topics to cover:

- Halal reputation
- Halal crisis
- The Halal Reputation Index
- Licence to Operate rating

Recommended literature:

- Tieman, M. (2017). Halal risk management: combining robustness and resilience. *Journal of Islamic Marketing*. Vol. 8 No. 3, pp. 461-475 DOI: https://doi.org/10.1108/JIMA-06-2015-0041
- Tieman, M. (2017). Halal reputation management: Combining individual and collective reputation management strategies. *Islam and Civilisational Renewal*. Vol. 8 No. 1, pp. 115-119
- Tieman, M. (2018). Licence to Operate in the Halal Market: A Matter of Alignment. *Islam and Civilisational Renewal* (ICR), Vol. 9 No. 3, pp. 390-393

- Tieman, M. (2019). Measuring corporate halal reputation: A corporate halal reputation index and research propositions. *Journal of Islamic Marketing*. Vol. 11 No. 3, pp. 591-601. DOI: https://doi.org/10.1108/JIMA-05-2018-0095

These ten lectures are supported by individual and group assignments. Site visits are highly recommended with halal-certified manufacturers, logistics service providers, hotels, or halal parks to be incorporated with a Halal Business Management course. The Halal Reputation GAME, developed by the author, is a key component of the Halal Business Excellence programme, providing university students and company executives an opportunity to learn halal reputation management by playing the Halal Reputation GAME.

Halal Reputation GAME

The Halal Reputation GAME was created to teach you to be the master of your halal reputation. How do the halal supply chain risk mitigation and recovery cycles work? What to do in different halal issue scenarios? What are the consequences of my choices for the corporate halal reputation and licence to operate?

Enquiries

For enquires regarding lecturing the Halal Business Management course, online Halal Business Management courses, Halal Business Management MasterClass, the Halal Reputation GAME, and other teaching materials and support, please contact us at: www.halalbusinessmanagement.com

APPENDIX 3

HALAL REPUTATION GAME

As shared in the book Halal Business Management, excellence in halal reputation management requires practise and repetition. Halal reputation is a journey, from regarding halal reputation management as a problem to be addressed urgently, viewing halal reputation as an asset, considering halal reputation as a competitive advantage that can increase sales, and representing halal reputation management in the boardroom. An imbalance with the halal market requirements, defined as the Licence To Operate (LTO) rating, directly affects your sales in Muslim markets.

The Halal Reputation GAME was created to teach you to be the master of your halal reputation.

For whom is the Halal Reputation GAME
- Brand owners: manufacturers, coffee chains, restaurant chains, hotel chains, retailers that are operating in or exporting to Muslim countries
- Universities and training institutes teaching students (and working adults) on halal business management
- Islamic organisations and halal certification bodies

Goal of the Halal Reputation GAME is to learn by doing:
- How do the halal supply chain risk mitigation and recovery cycles work?
- What to do in different halal issue scenarios?
- What are the consequences of my choices for the corporate halal reputation and licence to operate?

Objectives (How to win)
1. **Highest halal reputation**: build a strong halal authenticity, use a trustworthy halal certification body, create the right messages by company and supply chain partners, and ensure positive messages by external stakeholders
2. **Highest licence to operate:** maintain a high LTO rating in Muslim markets through both internal and external alignment

Use your Halal Advisor card with caution as you have only one per team.

Playing the halal reputation game

How to set up the game

1. Select a person to act as **Halal Certification Body**. This can be the lecturer/trainer
2. Place the cards on the table for ROUND 1 only
3. Divide the participants into teams of 3-7 persons max
4. Each team will take a one (1) **COMPANY CARD** and one (1) **HALAL ADVISOR CARD**

ROUND 1: Building your halal reputation
1. Each team chooses two (2) **HALAL REPUTATION ACTION CARDS**
2. Each Team details the Halal Reputation Strategy on the **HALAL REPUTATION SHEET**
3. Each Team decides to pull or not to pull the **HALAL ADVISOR CARD**
4. The Halal Certification Body distributes to each team a **CHANCE CARD**
5. Each Team calculates the scores of their team

ROUND 2: A halal issue
1. The Halal Certification Body distributes to each team a **HALAL ISSUE CARD**
2. Each Team details the mitigation response on the **HALAL REPUTATION SHEET**
3. Each Team decides to pull or not to pull the **HALAL ADVISOR CARD**
4. The Halal Certification Body distributes to each team a **CHANCE CARD**
5. Each Team calculates the scores of their team

ROUND 3: A halal crisis
1. The Halal Certification Body distributes to each team a **HALAL CRISIS CARD**

2. Each Team details the recovery response on the **HALAL REPUTATION SHEET**
3. Each Team decides to pull or not to pull the **HALAL ADVISOR CARD**
4. Meet your Halal Certification Body for help. The Halal Certification Body role is to assist you in diagnosis and decides if the issue is resolved (**GREEN CARD**) or not (**RED CARD**)
5. Each Team calculates the scores of their team

The winning team is the team with the highest Halal Reputation Index (HRI) and Licence To Operate (LTO) rating in round 3.

YOU ARE NOW READY TO PLAY THE HALAL REPUTATION GAME?

To order the game, please contact us at www.halalbusinessmanagement.com.

ABOUT THE AUTHOR

Marco Tieman is the founder and Chief Executive Officer of LBB International, a supply chain strategy consultancy and research firm. He has been an advisor to businesses and governments on halal industry strategy, halal assurance systems, halal supply chain management, halal cluster development, and halal risk and reputation management. He has been the project director responsible for the master plan and implementation of Modern Halal Valley, Indonesia's first and largest halal cluster.

He is a professor at Help University and a research fellow with the Universiti Malaya Halal Research Centre in Malaysia, conducting research in halal purchasing, halal supply chain management, and halal risk and reputation management. He completed his PhD on 'the application of halal in supply chain management: principles in the design and management of halal food supply chains'. He won academic awards for his research in halal purchasing and halal supply chain management. He is a member of the Senior Editorial Advisory Board of the Journal of Islamic Marketing (Emerald, United Kingdom).

He has an MSc in Industrial Engineering and Management Science from the University of Twente (the Netherlands) and a PhD in Business Management from the Universiti Teknologi MARA (Malaysia). In his free time, he enjoys walking, sailing, and listening to jazz music.

INDEX

0-base assessment 23, 24, 26–7, 29

activity outsourcing 62–3, 69
acquired halal asset 116, 119
additives, *see* food additives
air cargo pallet 77, 80, 142
airline 74
alcohol 21, 22, 65, 84, 85, 110, 135, 164
alignment 160, 167–9, 171
Al Islami Food 117
alliance network 43
allocation of halal cargo 78–9
Almarai 117
ambiguity 57, 66–7
America 11, 94
animal origin 11, 154
animal slaughter 11, 111
animal welfare 11
Arabic terms XIX
Aramco 116
Asia 7, 122
asset heavy 71–2
associations 14, 118
audit, *see* halal audit
Australia 11

Belgium 72
blockchains, *see* halal blockchains
blockchain technology 49, 52
bottleneck product 59–61, 68
BPJPH 19
branding halal 110–4
brand owner 51, 70, 165

Brunei 34, 35
bulk 35, 44, 146
bundling 48
business strategy 33

Cadbury 156–158
category 5, 56, 83–4, 127–8
certification, *see* halal certification
chain of custody 40
Chemical company of Malaysia 117
cigarettes 84–5
classification of halal logistics service providers 71–2
cleaning of transport 78–9
cleansing, *see* ritual cleansing
cluster management organisation 93, 102
clustering 88–90
Coca-Cola 99, 159
co-branding 159
co-creation 14, 121
coding 78, 80
coffee 95–6
collective halal reputation management 162–3
command and control 14, 73
commodity category 56, 58
commodity strategy 58
connectivity 162, 167
consolidation 36, 51, 83, 93
container 77, 80, 142
contamination, *see* cross-contamination
contract 57, 61, 67, 142
contracting 64, 67
contract clause 41
control 18

control measure 34
control of halal chains 11–3
cool chain 35, 44, 146
cooperative 62
corona crisis 63, 89
corporate halal reputation, *see* halal reputation
corporate reputation 86, 113, 162
coupling of brands 159
crisis management 63
critical path 26
cross-contamination 34–6, 84, 143, 146, 163–4
cross-docking 75, 77
cross-functional team 57, 149–51, 161
customer order fulfilment 41–2
customer service objectives 39
cyber-attacks 49

Danone 117
data security 49
DB Schenker 63, 73
DHL 73, 159
design principles 43–4
determine specifications 64–5
dietary guidelines 5
direct process activities 123
distribution 23
DNA, *see* halal DNA
documentation audit 28–9
doubt 34
dry chain 35, 44, 146

ecologically fitting supply chain 96
economies of chains 96
education 14, 18, 91–3
effectiveness 42
efficient 35, 42
Emirates 116–7
enablers 91, 97
energy 95

Europe 11, 19, 20–1, 94
Evans, Abdalhamid xvii, xviii, 4
evolution of halal 9
expediting and evaluation 64, 68
external stakeholder 14

facility design 24, 27
facility layout 28
fatwa xix, 21–2, 34, 49, 84, 91, 164
farm 95
farming clusters 11
first-tier supplier 37
first-tier customer 37
flavours 25
follow-up and evaluation 64, 68
food additives 11–2, 61, 65, 89, 95, 97, 103
food security 11
food shortages 12
food ingredients 11–2, 18, 21, 25, 37, 55–7, 61, 65, 89, 95, 97, 103
foundation of halal supply chain management 33–4
fourth-party logistics service provider 46, 63, 73
fragrances 25
France 117

franchise formula 62
FrieslandCampina 99

gambling 57, 66–7, 134
Garuda Indonesia 116
Germany 60
good, *see* tayyib
green material 26

Hajj 47, 63
halal xix, 3–10, 13
halal Aceh 94
halal act 19, 114
halal asset 46, 51, 130, 136
halal assurance activities 123
halal assurance system (HAS) 17–30, 66, 68, 73, 130, 141, 145, 148
halal assurance system documentation 23–4, 27–9
halal assurance system requirements 18
halal audit 24, 28, 126, 128, 148, 149
halal authenticity 109–10, 112, 119, 160, 164, 166–8, 170
halal authority 11, 29
halal blockchains 49–51
halal brand 24, 81, 89, 111, 117–9
halal brand equity assets 114–7, 119
halal brand positioning 117–8
halal brand positioning matrix 117, 119

halal branding 92, 107–20, 175
halal business management education 181–90
halal cargo box 46, 147
halal category, *see* category
halal certificate 34, 54, 66, 68, 70, 108, 163
halal certification 5, 12, 23–9, 53, 173
halal certification body (HCB) 18–25, 29, 39, 50, 66, 91, 93–4, 107–8, 111, 141, 160–1, 167
halal certification information checklist 178–80
halal certification programme 24, 133
halal cluster 45, 88–104
halal cluster model 91, 103
Halal cluster network 102–3
halal cluster organisation 101
halal co-branding 112–4, 119
halal coding 111–2, 114, 119
halal committee 18, 24, 27–8, 39–40, 54–5, 166–7
halal commodity 115, 119
halal commodity category 56
halal compliance 56
halal compliance matrix 56
halal compliant 54
halal compliant terminal 71–2, 74, 80–3
halal compliant terminal process 81
halal container 78
halal control measure 41–3, 71, 75–83, 130, 147
halal control point 41, 43, 71, 75–83, 130, 147
halal crisis 14, 151–2, 156, 163–5

halal crisis management 161, 167
halal diets 5, 6–7
halal disclosure laws 13
halal DNA 9, 123, 160
halal Dubai 94
halal ecosystem 89–90, 101, 103, 169
halal Europe 20–1
halal excellence philosophy 13–5, 177
halal-exclusive retailer 84–5, 87
halal expert 27–9, 151
halal image 166
halal incident 141, 151, 161
halal Indonesia 94
halal industry 5, 10–1, 15
halal industry strategy 90
halal ingredient branding 111, 114, 119
halal integrity 35, 37, 41–3, 70, 144, 158
halal integrity network 91, 93–4
halal issue 14, 49–50, 156, 165
halal issue classification 163–4
halal issue management 50, 161, 167
halal Johor 94
halal logistics 38, 66, 91–3
halal logistics and retailing 70–87
halal logistics asset 42, 147
halal logistics service provider 70–4

halal logistics/supply chain standard 73–4
halal logo 8, 107–8, 110–1, 119, 163
halal Malaysia 94, 98–100
halal management team, *see* halal committee
halal market requirements 168, 171
halal marketing 92, 121–37, 175
halal marketing channel 124–9
halal marketing strategy 121–9
halal maturity 10, 160, 167
halal maturity checklist 10
halal Medina 94
halal-mixed retailer 85–7
halal park 93, 97–104
halal performance 42–3
halal policy (statement) 18, 24–5, 38–9, 54–5, 57–8, 65–6, 160
halal product 8–9, 117–9
halal procurement maturity 53–8
halal procurement maturity model 54–5
halal procurement strategy 58–61
halal production chains 45
halal purchasing 53–69, 92
halal purchasing process 64–8
halal purchasing function 58
halal purchasing team 55, 57
halal regional distribution centre (HRDC) 72, 74, 93
halal retailing 83–7
halal reputation 14, 42, 122, 156–63, 169, 170
halal reputation game 190, 191–4
halal reputation index (HRI) 14, 42, 166–7, 171
halal reputation journey 170

halal reputation management 10–1, 91, 141, 156–72, 176
halal reputation strategy 161–3, 167
halal risk intensity 153–4
halal risk management 10–1, 73, 91, 141–55, 176
halal risk management control 143–5, 154
halal risk mitigation and communication plan 143, 149–50, 152–3, 161
halal risk recovery and communication plan 143, 152–3, 161
halal Saudi Arabia 94
halal scandal 162
halal security 144
halal-segregated retailer 84–5, 87
halal sensitive product 59–61
halal services marketing 129–33
halal slaughter, *see* ritual slaughter
halal standard 5, 22, 24, 28, 55, 57, 67, 74, 94, 169
halal standard operating procedures (SOPs) 40–1
halal status 40, 82
halal storage 82
halal strategy 23–5, 160, 167, 169
halal supplier selection iceberg 66–7
halal supply chain 8, 9, 33–52, 55, 91, 94–6

halal supply chain code 40, 46, 48, 67, 80, 82
halal supply chain control tower 72–4, 93
halal supply chain definitions 38
halal supply chain design principles 44
halal supply chain management 33–6, 38, 92, 174
halal supply chain model 36–44, 52, 146–7, 174
halal supply chain network 37, 46, 51, 151
halal supply chain orchestrator 45
halal supply chain risk mitigation cycle 145, 149–50
halal supply chain risk prevention cycle 145–8
halal supply chain risk profile 153–4
halal supply chain risk recovery cycle 145, 152–3
halal synergy 44, 52, 90, 102
halal trade 91
halal transport 71–2, 74, 78–80, 82, 93
halal transport process 78
halal trust 107–10, 119, 135, 145, 151
halal trust iceberg 109–10
halal trust measurement 110–11
halal UAE 94
halal value chain 8, 9, 48, 55, 122–3
halal value network 123–4
halal warehouse 71–2, 74–7, 93
halal warehouse process 75
halal zone 93, 97–104
halal zoning 28
haram xix, 5, 33–4, 51
HDC 98–9
hero 7–8
horizontal collaboration 41, 43–4, 46–8, 51–2, 58, 61–4, 69, 90, 93, 143, 147, 152–3, 169
Hofstede onion diagram 7–8

ihsan xix, 4, 95, 108, 110, 119
Implementation 23–4, 28–9
Indirect process activities 123
Indofood 117
Indonesia 8, 19, 72, 111, 116–7
information 18, 40, 48
information technology 49
inspection 68, 76, 81, 83
integrator 46
interest 57, 66–7
internal awareness campaign 54
internal halal audit 18
internal halal auditor 27–8, 39, 92, 148
ingredients, *see* food ingredients
insurance, *see* takaful
IOI 115
Islamic banking and finance 8–9, 12, 55, 57, 66, 91, 97, 103
Islamic slaughtering 8
Islamic values 3, 23, 91, 115, 145, 151, 169

JAKIM 19, 84, 98, 100, 112, 157, 164
joint procurement team 62, 69

kiblah XIX, 132
key performance indicator (KPI) 14, 166
KFC 111, 117
Kingdom of Saudi Arabia 47, 94, 116–7
kosher 112, 143
Kraljic, Peter 58
Kraljic portfolio matrix 59–61

labelling 18, 78, 80, 111
labelling law 13, 114
laboratory tests 29
last-mile 85
lawful, *see* halal
LBB International 166
lead-time 43, 94
Lembaga Tabung Haji 99–100
leverage product 59–61, 68
licence to operate 24, 70, 74
licence to operate (LTO) rating 14, 42, 168–71
livestock 79–80, 82–3
loading in transport 78–80
logistics control 39–40
logistics objectives 39
logistics service provider 50, 70, 126, 142–3
logo, *see* halal logo
L'Oréal 117

machine slaughter 48, 56
made in Europe 72
made in Saudi Arabia 72
Malaysia 8, 35, 72, 85, 115–8, 130, 156–7
managed process link 41, 150, 152–3
management review 18
manufacturer 50–1
manufacturing flow management 41–2
market qualifier 74, 112
market segmentation 122
marketing channel performance metrics 125–8
marketing mistakes 133–6
marketplace 63
Marshall, Alfred 88
material flow 27
materials handling 18, 23, 29
McDonald's 62, 111, 117, 130, 159
Media 162, 165, 169
medium najis xix
megatrends 10–1
messages 161–2, 166–8, 170–1
Middle East 7, 8, 122
mitigation 145, 148–50
mizan xix, 14, 95
Modern halal valley 95, 101–3
monitoring 147–50
moisture 35
Muslim company 8–9
Muslim consumer 91–2
Muslim-friendly hotel 129, 131–2

najis xix
Nestlé 116–7
Netherlands 72
network 145, 151
New Zealand 11
Nichirei Corporation 73

Nippon Express 73
niyyah xix, 25, 39, 109–10, 119, 169
non-asset based 71–2
non-compliance 163–4
non-conformance 18
non-halal xix

OneAgrix 63
operational control tower 63
operational purchasing process 64, 69
ordering 64, 67
order picking 75, 77
order winner 74
organisation 18, 40
Organisation of Islamic Cooperation (OIC) 12, 19, 100, 115
organic 13
over-branding 112–3

packed in Europe 72
packed in Saudi Arabia 72
perception 34, 36, 51, 84, 113, 146, 163–4
performance measurement 51
Petronas 116
phasing of halal brands 24
point of parity 118
pooling 48
pork 84, 110, 134, 164
Porter, Michael 88–90, 123
potential halal asset 115, 119
practical 35
practice and repetition 14
prevention 145–8

primary packaging 18, 34–5, 37, 56, 65
process 18
process approach 4, 15
process quality 42
procurement strategy 55, 57–8
product approach 4, 15, 71, 89
product recall 50
production 18, 23, 29, 91
project purchasing team 62–3, 69
public recall 50
purchasing 23, 29, 41–2, 53
purchasing contract 55
purchasing function 54
purchasing process 55, 57, 58
pursuit of excellence 4, 173–71
putaway 75–6

Qatar 116
Qatar Airways 116
quality assurance activities 123
quality management system (QMS) 18–9, 66, 73
quarantine area 28, 68, 76, 83
Quran xx, 4, 6, 7, 8, 91, 131

Ramadan 7, 135
Receiving 75–6
Recovery 145, 151–3
red item management 24, 26, 29

red material 26
reputation management 9
research 91–3, 103
resilience 144–5, 149, 152–4
retailer 50–1, 96, 142–3
risks 40
risk management 9
risk profile, see halal supply chain risk profile
risk of contamination 33–4, 36, 51, 84, 146
risk vulnerability assessment 146
rituals 7–8
ritual cleansing 8, 34, 65, 79
ritual slaughter 8, 12, 21, 65
robustness 43, 144–5, 147, 153–4
routine items 26
routine product 59–61

Saudia 116
second-tier customer 37
second-tier supplier 37
select supplier 64–7
sertu xx
severe najis xx, 44, 79–80, 82
shared ledger 50
shariah xx, 4, 35
shariah-compliant hotel 129, 131–2
shipping 75, 77
shipping line 74
Sime Darby 115
Singapore 19
smart contract 49–50
Spain 72
Spar 62
speculation, see gambling
standard, see halal standard

standardisation 46, 51
Starbucks 116, 130
storage 18, 75–6
strategic alliances 14
strategic product 59–61, 68
stunning 48, 56
sunnah xx
supermarket 110–1
supplier 50
supplier audit 54
supplier management 68
supplier rating 68
supplier visit 29
supply chain activities 71–2
supply chain approach 15, 71, 89
supply chain control tower 62–3, 69
supply chain costs 42, 94
supply chain execution 50
supply chain network structure 40–1
supply chain business processes 41
supply chain objectives 38–9
supply chain optimisation 46
supply chain processes 71–2
supply chain partner classification 41
supply chain resources 40
supply chain visibility 73
Switzerland 117
symbol 7, 8
synergy 44, 51–2, 61, 101, 115

tactical purchasing process 64, 69
takaful 57, 66, 97

tayyib xx, 4, 13
team 14
Thailand 19
third-party logistics service provider 46, 48, 63, 72–4
traceability 18, 49
tracking and tracing 40
training 14, 18, 24, 28, 40, 54, 92, 130, 133, 169
transparency 51, 108, 110, 119
transport 18
trust 4, 93, 107, 160, 166–8, 170
Turkey 116
Turkish Airlines 116

UAE 116, 117
Unilever 117
United Kingdom 117
USA 117
umrah 63
unitised 35, 146

unit load device 77, 80, 142
universities 92
utilisation 43

value-added logistics 51, 75, 77, 93
value chain approach 15, 89
values 8
Van Weele purchasing process 64
vertical collaboration 41, 43–6, 51–2, 90, 93, 143, 147, 152–3
vulnerability 147

Wardah 111, 117
waste 42, 95
water management 95
waqf 97

yellow material 26